EVERY DAY
AMAZING

First published in Great Britain In 2021
by Laurence King Publishing

1 3 5 7 9 10 8 6 4 2

Text © Mike Barfield 2021
Illustrations © Marianna Madriz 2021

Mike Barfield has asserted his right under the
copyright, designs and patents act 1988, to be identified
as the author of this work.

A CIP catalog record for this book is available
from the British Library.

ISBN 978-1-91394-704-0

Printed and bound in China

Laurence King Publishing
An imprint of
Hachette Children's Group
Part of Hodder and Stoughton
Carmelite House
50 Victoria Embankment
London EC4Y 0DZ

An Hachette UK Company
www.hachette.co.uk
www.hachettechildrens.co.uk

www.laurenceking.com

Laurence King Publishing is committed to ethical
and sustainable production. We are proud participants
in The Book Chain Project® bookchainproject.com

ACKNOWLEDGMENTS

This book owes a deep debt of gratitude to Sir Tim Berners-Lee
(see June 8th and August 6th), whose development of the
World Wide Web makes it possible for date-based fact fans
like the author to tap into online encyclopedias, newspaper
archives, history sites, diaries, and other daily digital
goldmines too numerous to list here. However, special
mention should be made of Scottish author and dictionary
compiler Robert Chambers, whose *Book of Days*, published
in 1864, is the great-granddaddy of all calendar-based trivia
collections. I offer big and sincere thanks to everyone who
goes about adding to the sum of fun human knowledge, but
this book is actually dedicated to my wife Jessica, the most
important date in my own life and every day amazing.

Mike Barfield

If it wasn't for the invention of television (August 18th)
and animation (August 17th) my childhood wouldn't have
been quite the same. So many characters and stories
inspired me to draw from an early age, and drove me to
illustrate books like the one you're holding in your hands
now! I hope this book also inspires you to seek even more
fun facts through history and to learn from them. I want
to dedicate this to my family, especially to my nephew
Alex. And of course, to my partner Sul (making a special
appearance as a pirate on September 19th)—thanks for
making me a better person every day.

Marianna Madriz

EVERY DAY

AMAZING

FANTASTIC FACTS FOR EVERY DAY OF THE YEAR

MIKE BARFIELD

Illustrations by **MARIANNA MADRIZ**

LAURENCE KING PUBLISHING

EVERY DAY IS AMAZING

No matter what day you are reading this, something amazing will have happened on the same day in the past—it could be an important discovery (January 5th), a comet sighting (May 18th), a regal journey (June 13th), or even some very famous footsteps (July 21st).

Or maybe a brand-new baby was born—a happy arrival that happens about 360,000 times every day on Earth. You were one of those once, and your amazing day is in this book, even if you were born in a leap year on February 29th.

But birthdays aren't the only reason for reading this book. Perhaps right now a nation is enjoying a favorite treat (October 4th), marking an important moment in history (November 11th), or celebrating its independence (December 29th).

Dip into these dates and you'll find time flying by as you skip from one incredible entry to another. As you are about to find out, every day really *is* amazing!

JANUARY

01
JANUARY

FIRST FOOT FORWARD

In Scotland, New Year is known as Hogmanay. In a tradition known as "first-footing," the first visitor to enter a home on January 1st should be a tall, dark-haired man and carry a gift, such as a lump of coal, to ensure good luck for the year ahead.

ARRIVALS
Pierre de Coubertin, French "father of the modern Olympic Games" (1863)

DEPARTURES
Hiram "Hank" Williams, American country and western music star (1953)

BACK TO FRONT

Since 1989, this has been Z Day—a rare opportunity for names and nations at the very end of the alphabet to be considered first for once. This is good news for African countries Zambia and Zimbabwe; people called Zoe, Zak, Zane, and Zara; and—of course—zombies.

02
JANUARY

ARRIVALS
Isaac Asimov, American sci-fi author (1920)

DEPARTURES
Guccio Gucci, Italian fashion designer (1953)

Say "Cheese!"

In 1839, French artist and inventor Louis Daguerre takes the first ever photograph of the moon. Daguerre developed an early form of photography, known as daguerreotypes, and recorded a crescent moon shining high over his native France. Sadly, the historic snap was lost in a fire just a few months later.

PURR-FECTION

Today, cats worldwide celebrate Happy Mew Year—a holiday invented specially for them back in 2016. Cat owners shower their moggies with cuddles, treats, titbits, and pure devotion—just as their pets expect every other day of the year too!

03
JANUARY

ARRIVALS
Greta Thunberg, Swedish climate activist (2003)

DEPARTURES
Joy Adamson, Austrian naturalist and *Born Free* author (1980)

SLUUUUURP!

This is Drinking Straw Day, celebrating the date in 1888 on which American inventor Marvin C. Stone patented his new device, the paper drinking straw. Before then, people sipped through short lengths of dried plant stems, which often added an odd "grassy" flavor to drinks.

04
JANUARY

Get Your Skates On!
The first four-wheeled roller skates are patented in the USA in 1863 by their inventor, James Plimpton. Plimpton's skates—the forerunner of all modern versions—have wooden wheels and are the first to enable the wearer to steer by simply leaning left or right.

LITTLE THINGS MEAN A LOT
Today is National Trivia Day, 24 hours in which to celebrate making space in your brain for fun facts, such as koalas and humans have almost identical fingerprints, and bananas are slightly radioactive. Enjoy!

05
JANUARY

LET THEM EAT CAKE!
This evening is Twelfth Night—the last of the twelve days of Christmas. In olden days, a special Twelfth Night cake was baked with a bean and a pea hidden inside. Whoever received a slice containing them became king or queen of the party for that night and ruled over all the other guests!

Ray of Hope
In 1896, newspapers announce the discovery of X-rays by German physicist Wilhelm Röntgen—the X stands for "unknown." Just weeks earlier, Röntgen had used his discovery to take the first ever medical X-ray: a photo of his wife's hand.

06
JANUARY

"Elementary!"
Fans of fictional sleuth Sherlock Holmes say he was born on this day in 1854, having used clues in the stories to work out the date. Created by British author Arthur Conan Doyle in November 1887, the detective remains as popular as ever and has been portrayed in movies more often than any other character.

07
JANUARY

Balloonatics!

The first balloon crossing of the English Channel occurs in 1785. Frenchman Jean-Pierre Blanchard and American John Jeffries lift off from the English port of Dover in a hydrogen-filled balloon and land in France 150 minutes later, but only after throwing out everything heavy—including Jean-Pierre's trousers!

ARRIVALS
Gerald Durrell, British author and conservationist (1925)

DEPARTURES
Nikola Tesla, Austrian-American inventor (1943)

Tipping Tower

In 1990, the Leaning Tower of Pisa—the bell tower of Pisa Cathedral in Italy—is closed to the public for the first time in 800 years due to fears it is about to fall over. After emergency repairs, it is reopened in 2001, and expected to be safe for at least another 200 years. Honest.

ROCK ON

Today is designated Old Rock Day. This is not a celebration of the music parents dance to when they think no one is looking, but a day created by scientists to promote rocks and fossils. The oldest rocks on Earth can be found in Canada and date back over four billion years!

08
JANUARY

ARRIVALS
Stephen Hawking, British physicist and author (1942)

DEPARTURES
Galileo Galilei, Italian astronomer (1642)

Coming Up!

In 1992, at a major state banquet in Tokyo, George H. W. Bush—then president of the USA—becomes ill and vomits in the lap of the Japanese prime minister, live on television. The woozy president then asks to be rolled under the table until the dinner is over.

IN A SPIN

This is Earth's Rotation Day. On this day in 1851, French scientist Léon Foucault proves that the Earth spins on its axis by hanging a heavy lead-filled brass ball on a wire 220 feet long, making a giant pendulum. The pendulum swings from side to side, but also travels slowly round in a circle as the Earth moves beneath it.

09
JANUARY

Not So Little Mermaids

In 1493, Italian explorer Christopher Columbus spots what he thinks are three mermaids off the coast of the Caribbean island of Dominica. He writes in his journal that they are "not half as beautiful as they are painted." However, he has probably seen a trio of manatees or "sea cows"—seal-like mammals with big eyes and bulbous bodies.

All of a Flutter

The Mountain of the Butterflies, the winter home of monarch butterflies, is discovered in 1975. The beautiful black and orange butterflies migrate thousands of miles each year across North America, but where they spent the winter was a mystery until two American zoologists found them in their millions in a forest in Mexico's Sierra Madre mountains.

ARRIVALS
Kate Middleton, British Duchess of Cambridge (1982)

DEPARTURES
Katherine Mansfield, New Zealand writer (1923)

10
JANUARY

Quiff of Danger

Tintin, the brave boy reporter and his faithful fox terrier sidekick, Snowy, make their debut in the Belgian children's newspaper *Le Petit Vingtième* (*The Little Twentieth*) in 1929. Created by cartoonist Hergé (real name Georges Remi), Tintin travels to Russia in the first of 24 adventures across five decades.

Going Underground

The world's first underground passenger railway opens in London in 1863. The line connects two major above-ground railway terminals, with passengers traveling in gas-lit carriages pulled by steam locomotives. Despite the engines filling the tunnels with thick smoke, 38,000 people use "the Tube" on its first day alone.

ARRIVALS
Barbara Hepworth, British sculptor (1903)

DEPARTURES
Coco Chanel, French fashion designer (1971)

11
JANUARY

PIP, PIP, HOORAY!

This is German Apples Day, an event started in 2010 to promote the many different varieties of the fruit grown in Germany. Thousands of apples are handed out on the streets of big cities, as well as being given free to schools and kindergartens, meaning everyone gets an apple—not just the teachers!

ARRIVALS
Mary J. Blige, American singer (1971)

DEPARTURES
Richmal Crompton, British *Just William* children's series author (1969)

12
JANUARY

ARRIVALS
Pixie Lott, British singer
(1991)

DEPARTURES
Agatha Christie, British
queen of crime fiction
(1976)

What a Stinker!

In 1960, the movie *Scent of Mystery* is released in the USA, the first to add smells to the cinema-going experience. Known as Smell-O-Vision, the process involves pumping out scents such as roses, pipe smoke, and freshly baked bread into the audience. Despite this, the movie is an expensive flop.

HAIRCUT, SIR?

Today is Yennayer, the start of the new year for the Berber people of the African country of Algeria, who trace their history back to the days of the Egyptian pharaohs. Yennayer is celebrated with special dishes made with couscous and other grains. Small boys also receive their first ever haircut on this day.

13
JANUARY

Disc World

Today in 1957, the Wham-O company of California launches its Pluto Platter, a plastic flying disc, soon renamed the Frisbee. The new name comes from the metal dishes produced by the Frisbie Pie Company which college students used to skim to each other.

Ride, Sally, Ride!

In 1978, the American space agency NASA selects its first ever female astronauts. The group of six women includes Sally Ride, who, five years later, becomes the first American woman to fly in space—and the third woman in space, overall. She says of her time above Earth: "The stars don't look bigger, but they do look brighter."

ARRIVALS
Michael Bond, British
Paddington Bear author
(1926)

DEPARTURES
Wyatt Earp, American
Wild West lawman (1929)

14
JANUARY

Reed All About It!

The clarinet is claimed to have been born on this day in 1690. It was invented by German musical instrument maker Johann Christoph Denner, who adds keys to a simpler instrument so it can play more notes.

ARRIVALS
Hugh Lofting, British
Doctor Doolittle author
(1886)

DEPARTURES
Lewis Carroll (real name
Charles Dodgson), British
Alice in Wonderland author
(1898)

15
JANUARY

Know It All

Wikipedia, the free online encyclopedia, is launched in 2001 by founders Jimmy Wales and Larry Sanger. The name is a combination of the Hawaiian word *wiki*—meaning "quick"—and the word *encyclopedia*. *Wikipedia* is written by its users, who occasionally post fake information: for example, the false claim that British soccer player David Beckham was a goalkeeper in China in the 18th century.

FRUITY

Today is Strawberry Day in Japan—chosen because the Japanese word for strawberry (*ichigo*) sounds like the two Japanese words *ichi* and *go*, meaning "one" and "five"—which together give the number 15. Delights on sale in Japanese stores include strawberry pancakes and strawberry and whipped cream sandwiches!

Top That

In 1797, John Hetherington causes alarm on the streets of London when he is seen sporting on his head a tall, shiny structure that is "calculated to frighten timid people"—or so it is claimed when he appears in court the next day. His crime is to have invented and worn in public the first ever top hat.

ARRIVALS
Martin Luther King Jr, American civil rights leader (1929)

DEPARTURES
Daisy Ashford, British author of *The Young Visiters*, written when she was just nine (1972)

16
JANUARY

Good Knight

Don Quixote, the Spanish book considered to be the first modern novel, was published in 1605. Written by Miguel de Cervantes, it has as its title character a make-believe knight who has crazy adventures in the countryside, including "tilting at windmills" with a lance—giving us the phrase still used for a pointless task.

ARRIVALS
Ruby Rube, British YouTube vlogger (2006)

DEPARTURES
Eugene Cernan, American astronaut and last man on the moon (2017)

NOTHING DOING

In the USA, this is National Nothing Day, intended to be the one day of the year when nothing is marked, honored, or celebrated. It was invented by San Francisco newspaper columnist Harold Pullman Coffin, who first proposed this "un-event" in 1972. However, the day itself has now become a celebration. Go figure!

17
JANUARY

ARRIVALS
Muhammad Ali,
American boxing legend
(1942)

DEPARTURES
T. H. White, British
author of *The Sword in
the Stone* (1964)

Kid's Stuff

Today is the birthday in 1706 of American scientist Benjamin Franklin, famous for having supposedly flown a kite in a storm to prove lightning was a form of electricity. (Never do this—it's madly dangerous!) At the age of 12, young Ben invented wooden swimming flippers, and to mark this, today is also Kid Inventors' Day.

Spinach's Biggest Fan

Popeye the Sailor made his first appearance in 1929, in a comic strip called *Thimble Theatre* by E. C. Segar. At first only a minor character, Popeye soon became the star. Originally, Popeye didn't get strength from eating spinach—instead, he got luck by rubbing the feathers of a magic hen called Bernice.

18
JANUARY

ARRIVALS
A. A. Milne, British
Winnie-the-Pooh author
(1882)

DEPARTURES
John Tyler, tenth
American president
(1862)

Cook's Tour

In 1778, British explorer Captain James Cook and his crew become the first Europeans to visit a string of islands in the northern Pacific Ocean. Cook calls them the Sandwich Islands, in honor of the Earl of Sandwich—the same person the bready snack is named after. Today the islands are known as Hawaii.

19
JANUARY

Freezy

Antarctica is claimed for the USA in 1840 by US explorer Charles Wilkes, though today it is an international zone. Antarctica is the fifth biggest continent and the coldest and windiest place on Earth. It is also technically a desert, as rain rarely falls. To date, only 11 babies have been born in Antarctica, the first being Argentinian Emilio Palma in 1978.

ARRIVALS
Nina Bawden, British
Carrie's War author
(1925)

DEPARTURES
Hedy Lamarr, Austrian-
American actor and
inventor (2000)

Cheesy

In 1973, artist Carl Andre displays 500 pounds of cottage cheese and 12 gallons of tomato ketchup in an art gallery in Washington DC, calling the exhibition *American Decay*. However, the smell of the putrid food proves so bad that the show closes the next day.

20 JANUARY

Hoop La!

The first official basketball game is played in a gymnasium in Springfield, Massachusetts, USA, in 1892. The game, invented by PE teacher James Naismith, uses a soccer ball and wooden fruit baskets attached to a balcony. The baskets still have bottoms, so each time a point is scored, someone has to retrieve the ball by hand.

ARRIVALS
Edwin "Buzz" Aldrin, American astronaut and second man on the moon (1930)

DEPARTURES
Audrey Hepburn, British actor (1993)

21 JANUARY

ARRIVALS
Christian Dior, French fashion designer (1905)

DEPARTURES
George Orwell, British *Animal Farm* author (1950)

HOLA!

This is Mariachi Day in Mexico. Mariachi music is characterized by musicians in highly decorative traditional rodeo outfits and sombrero hats playing guitars, trumpets, and violins. Bands play at both weddings and funerals, and many Mexican girls have a mariachi band perform on their fifteenth birthday.

TV Dinner

The world's first TV cookery show is broadcast live by the BBC in 1937. Called *Cook's Night Out*, it is hosted by celebrated French chef Marcel Boulestin, who shows viewers his way to make an omelet.

22 JANUARY

Big Cheese

Work on the world's largest cheese finishes in Denmark, Wisconsin, USA, in 1964. The humungous cheddar is made from more than 42,000 gallons of milk and weighs over 16 tons. It is transported on a giant tractor-trailer dubbed the Cheesemobile so it can be displayed at the New York World's Fair.

ARRIVALS
John Hurt, British actor who played Ollivander in the *Harry Potter* movies (1940)

DEPARTURES
Queen Victoria, British monarch and empress (1901)

Big Apple

The first Apple Macintosh personal computer is introduced to the world in 1984 with a high-budget TV advert broadcast during the American football Super Bowl game. The Macintosh is named after the favorite variety of apple—the McIntosh—munched by one of the company's employees.

13

23
JANUARY

Far from Home

In 2003, the final radio signal is received on Earth from space probe Pioneer 10, now about 7½ billion miles away. Launched in 1972, the spacecraft was the first artificial object to leave our solar system, and carries a metal plaque with information about Earth, in case it is encountered by other intelligent life forms.

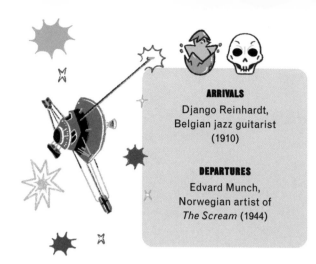

ARRIVALS
Django Reinhardt, Belgian jazz guitarist (1910)

DEPARTURES
Edvard Munch, Norwegian artist of *The Scream* (1944)

24
JANUARY

ARRIVALS
Hadrian, Roman emperor and wall builder (76 CE)

DEPARTURES
Winston Churchill, British wartime leader (1965)

LITTLE THINGS

Today sees the start of the Alasitas Fair in La Paz, Bolivia. Stalls sell tiny models of household items such as food, mobile phones, and tools, which are bought and given as gifts. The hope is that Ekeko, the local god of luck and abundance, will then provide the real things for recipients. (Little) fingers crossed!

All Over Now

In 1972, Japanese army sergeant Shoichi Yokoi is found hiding in the jungle on the Pacific island of Guam, over 25 years after the end of the Second World War. Apparently, Yokoi knew that the war was over but continued to believe that his life was in danger.

25
JANUARY

Ice Queen

The first Olympic Winter Games open in Chamonix, France, in 1924. One of the competitors in the ladies' figure skating is 11-year-old Norwegian Sonja Henie. Sonja comes last but wins gold medals in the next three Winter Olympics, and also becomes a Hollywood film star.

MR BURNS

The Scots celebrate Burns Night with a special supper in memory of national poet, Robert "Rabbie" Burns, born this day in 1759. Kilts are worn, speeches are made, and a bagpiper plays as a plump haggis is brought into the room. After more poetry, the haggis is toasted with whisky and devoured.

ARRIVALS
John Cooper Clarke, British poet (1949)

DEPARTURES
Alphonse "Al" Capone, American gangster (1947)

26 JANUARY

G'DAY

Today is Australia Day, marking the arrival of the First Fleet of British ships in 1788. Some celebrate with festivities and fireworks, though many indigenous Australians instead consider this the date their ancient homeland was invaded.

What a Gem!

The largest gem-quality diamond ever found is discovered in a mine in South Africa in 1905. Named the Cullinan Diamond, it is the size of a child's fist. It is cut into 105 stones, the two largest of which now form part of the British Crown Jewels, securely guarded in the Tower of London.

27 JANUARY

Light Bulb Moment

In 1880, American inventor Thomas Alva Edison is granted US Patent 223,898 for an incandescent electric lamp. As a result, Edison is now commonly credited with producing the first light bulb, even though his British rival Joseph Swan had lit a street with electric bulbs the previous year. The debate still goes on.

FLUSHED WITH SUCCESS

Americans in particular enjoy celebrating Thomas Crapper Day—this being the day in 1910 on which the successful British plumber and inventor died. Many mistakenly believe Crapper invented the flushing toilet. He didn't, though he did invent the ballcock—the floating device inside a toilet cistern that ends the refill.

28 JANUARY

Not So Fast!

The world's first speeding ticket is issued in 1896 to Walter Arnold of Kent, UK. Not only is he caught driving four times the speed limit of 2 miles per hour, he also fails to have someone walking in front of his vehicle with a red warning flag.

Snow Joke!

The largest ever recorded snowflake falls in Fort Keogh, Montana, USA, in 1887. The flake measures over 15 inches in diameter and is some 8 inches thick. Imagine catching that on your tongue!

29
JANUARY

Happy Brrm-day!

The automobile was born today in 1886. German engineer Karl Benz filed a patent in Berlin for Motor-Car No 1—a petrol-engined cross between a tricycle and a horse-drawn buggy. With a top speed of nearly 10 miles per hour, No 1 had its first public outing five months later, Benz's teenage son Eugen walking alongside it with extra fuel.

ARRIVALS
Oprah Winfrey, American TV host (1954)

DEPARTURES
King George III, British monarch (1820)

30
JANUARY

ARRIVALS
Olivia Colman, British actor (1974)

DEPARTURES
Mahatma Gandhi, Indian politician and activist (1948)

DOUGH!

This is National Croissant Day in the USA—though, of course, every day is croissant day in France. Croissants were invented by former Austrian Army officer August Zang, who opened a bakery selling the curvy confections in Paris in 1839. Popular today is the cronut—a cross between a croissant and a donut.

31
JANUARY

Paws for Thought

In 1867, four large bronze lions around Nelson's Column in Trafalgar Square, London, are finally revealed to the public. They were designed by artist Edwin Landseer, who had a dead lion sent to his studio to copy. However, it rotted so quickly that the paws of his statues are actually based on those of domestic cats, not lions.

Monkeying About

In 1963, American cartoonist Don Martin draws a crazy comic strip in which a man wears a gorilla suit all day. Though no date is mentioned in the story, fans of Martin's work now celebrate January 31st as National Gorilla Suit Day. They must be bananas!

ARRIVALS
Justin Timberlake, American singer (1981)

DEPARTURES
A. A. Milne, British *Winnie-the-Pooh* author (1956)

FEBRUARY

01
FEBRUARY

SPRING THING

In old Ireland and Scotland, the ancient Gaelic festival of Imbolc is celebrated to mark the start of spring. However, good weather on this day is considered an ill omen, as it means the mythical Queen of Winter is out gathering more sticks for her fire and spring will be delayed.

ARRIVALS
Harry Styles, British One Direction singer (1994)

DEPARTURES
Mary Shelley, British *Frankenstein* author (1851)

La La Land

In 1887, shoemaker-turned-estate agent Harvey Wilcox registers plans for a new settlement to be built on some land he owns in Southern California, having failed to grow fruit on it. His wife, Daeida, names the new estate Hollywood, though the famous giant white-lettered sign won't be erected until 1923.

02
FEBRUARY

Pipe Down

The Pompidou Centre, a huge art gallery and cultural center, opens to the public in Paris in 1977. The building is uncompromisingly modern, with all its plumbing, air conditioning, and wiring on show in tubes on the outside.

ARRIVALS
Hamnet Shakespeare, British, William Shakespeare's son, baptized (1585)

DEPARTURES
Gene Kelly, American musical actor (1996)

Rescued!

In 1709, a Scottish castaway called Alexander Selkirk was rescued after over four years marooned alone on a remote island off the coast of Chile. Selkirk survived by hunting wild animals and making clothes from the skins of wild goats—inspiring author Daniel Defoe to write the book *Robinson Crusoe*.

DAY AFTER DAY

Today is Groundhog Day at Gobbler's Knob in the town of Punxsutawney, Philadelphia, USA. If Punxsutawney Phil, a large furry rodent, emerges from his burrow and sees his shadow, winter will last another six weeks. Thanks to the hit movie *Groundhog Day* (1993), Phil is now a film star!

03
FEBRUARY

Stick with It

In 1877, a musical composition with the title *The Celebrated Chop Waltz* is registered in London. It is credited to "Arthur de Lulli," but is actually written by a 16-year-old girl called Euphemia Allen. Her piano piece is now better known as *Chopsticks*.

ARRIVALS
Warwick Davis, British *Star Wars* and *Harry Potter* movies actor (1970)

DEPARTURES
Buddy Holly, American rock 'n' roll singer (1959)

BEAN HAVING FUN?

Today is Setsubun in Japan, the day before the beginning of spring. In a traditional ritual called *mamemaki,* people cleanse their houses of the past year by throwing roasted soybeans out of the door while shouting: "Demons out! Luck in!" The door is then slammed shut.

04
FEBRUARY

ARRIVALS
Rosa Parks, American civil rights activist (1913)

DEPARTURES
Satyendra Nath Bose, Indian physicist after whom subatomic particle the boson is named (1974)

Thumbs Up?

In 2004, 19-year-old Harvard University student Mark Zuckerberg launches an online directory of fellow students, calling it TheFacebook. A year later, it becomes simply Facebook, and grows into a global social networking phenomenon. Zuckerberg's personal wealth is said to be over $70 billion. Would you "like" that?

YES OR NO?

This is National Day in Sri Lanka—a name meaning "resplendent island." In 1960, the small teardrop-shaped nation elected the world's first female prime minister. Today it is a major holiday spot, though visitors can get a little confused: Sri Lankans shake their heads to say "Yes," rather than nod!

05
FEBRUARY

ARRIVALS
Cristiano Ronaldo, Portuguese soccer star (1985)

DEPARTURES
Granny Dakshayani, famous 88-year-old Indian elephant (2019)

NUTTY IDEA

Since 2007, this is World Nutella Day, started by a fan of the hazelnut and cocoa spread. The sweet treat was launched in 1964 and is so popular that in 2015 a French judge had to stop two parents from naming their baby girl Nutella, because he thought she would be teased.

06
FEBRUARY

KIWI CULTURE

This is Waitangi Day in New Zealand, a national commemoration of a treaty signed in 1840 between British settlers and native Maori chiefs. Various aspects of Maori culture are celebrated, including traditional *waka* canoes, wood-carving, tattooing, and performances of the *haka*—their tongue-tastic ceremonial dance.

ARRIVALS
Bob Marley, Jamaican reggae superstar (1945)

DEPARTURES
Joseph Priestley, British chemist who discovered oxygen (1804)

Very Fishy

In 1989, residents of Ipswich, Queensland, Australia, were rather surprised to find hundreds of sardine-sized fish raining down on them. The fish had been lifted from the sea by freak weather conditions before hurtling to earth. Luckily, they weren't in cans.

07
FEBRUARY

Whale of a Time

In 2007, British yachtswoman Ellen MacArthur sailed into history by completing a massive 31,480-mile round-the-world voyage in just 71 days, 14 hours, and 18 minutes (still a world record for the distance covered). During her time at sea she had to cope with rough weather, a damaged sail, and almost hitting a whale.

ARRIVALS
Laura Ingalls Wilder, American *Little House on the Prairie* author (1867)

DEPARTURES
Adolphe Sax, Belgian saxophone inventor (1894)

SPICE IT UP

Today is Independence Day in Grenada, a day celebrated with many parades and people dressing in the national colors of red, gold, and green. The Caribbean island is a major producer of nutmeg. The crop is so important to Grenada that a nutmeg pod features on its flag.

08
FEBRUARY

Still Missing

Shergar, one of the world's most successful racehorses, is stolen from a stud farm in Ireland in 1983. The horse, valued at around $15 million, was taken by armed robbers who then demanded a ransom of $3 million for his return. No money was paid, and poor Shergar was never seen again.

ARRIVALS
Jules Verne, French science fiction writer (1828)

DEPARTURES
Charles Wilkes, American Antarctic explorer (1877)

09
FEBRUARY

Net Gain

Volleyball is invented in 1895 in Holyoke, Massachusetts, USA, by physical education instructor William G. Morgan as a gentler game for people who find basketball too rough. Copying the net used in badminton, Morgan originally called his new sport Mintonette, and teams could have as many players as they wished on court!

SLICE OF THE ACTION

Today is National Pizza Day, a celebration of the tasty cheese and tomato treat. Its origins go back to Naples, Italy, but today pizza has taken over the planet. Pepperoni tops the topping charts, with some of the weirdest additions being mashed potato, chocolate, smoked reindeer, and crocodile.

10
FEBRUARY

Reel Clever

In 1943, American war worker Vesta Stoudt writes to her nation's president outlining an idea she has had for a strong, waterproof fabric-backed sticky tape that could be used to seal boxes of ammunition. The president loves the idea, and soon afterwards the first ever reels of duct tape are being manufactured.

Check, Mate!

In 1996, a computer called Deep Blue becomes the first machine to beat a reigning world chess champion. Russian chess grandmaster Garry Kasparov loses the first of six games to Deep Blue, but recovers to win 4–2 overall. A year later they have a rematch, and this time Deep Blue wins and promptly retires.

11
FEBRUARY

GO GIRL!

Today is the International Day of Women and Girls in Science—created by the United Nations to encourage more females into the fields of science and technology. Despite low numbers, the only person so far to have won the Nobel Prize in two different sciences is French-Polish Marie Curie—a woman!

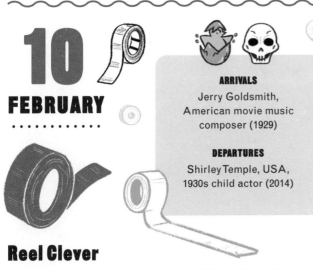

12
FEBRUARY

ARRIVALS
Judy Blume, American
children's author (1938)

DEPARTURES
Charles Schulz, American
cartoonist and *Charlie
Brown and Snoopy* creator
(2000)

The Origin of Darwin

Naturalist Charles Darwin was born today in 1809, an event celebrated as Darwin Day. Darwin famously outlined his theory of evolution in his 1859 work *On the Origin of Species*, but he was also an expert on beetles, barnacles, coral reefs, and earthworms!

Tunnel Vision

In 1994, 118 people set off from France on a charity walk to the UK through the Channel Tunnel, led by British Olympic athlete Daley Thompson. This is the first time anyone has walked to the UK from mainland Europe since the last Ice Age, about 10,000 years ago.

13
FEBRUARY

ARRIVALS
Robbie Williams, British
pop singer (1974)

DEPARTURES
Christabel Pankhurst,
British women's rights
activist (1958)

Lost Opportunity

Covered in dust, and 124 million miles from Earth, the US Mars rover Opportunity finally completes its 15-year mission in 2019. In this time, Oppy, as it is nicknamed, has climbed mountains, discovered the first Martian meteorite, and traveled 18 miles over the rocky surface of the red planet.

14
FEBRUARY

Going Viral

Video-sharing site YouTube launches in 2005. The first video is uploaded five weeks later and features one of YouTube's co-founders standing in front of elephants at a zoo, commenting that "they have really, really, really long trunks." To date, it has had more than 80 million views.

ARRIVALS
Freddie Highmore,
British *Charlie and the
Chocolate Factory*
actor (1992)

DEPARTURES
Dolly the Sheep,
the first successfully
cloned adult animal
(2003)

LOVE ME DO

Valentine's Day is named after one or more saints, none of whom we know much about, but all of whom met rather grisly ends centuries ago. The skull of one of them (possibly) sits in a gilded glass case in a church in Rome. It is decorated with a garland of flowers, but still doesn't look romantic.

15
FEBRUARY

ARRIVALS
Matt Groening, American creator of *The Simpsons* (1954)

DEPARTURES
Socrates, ancient Greek philosopher, sentenced to death (399 BCE)

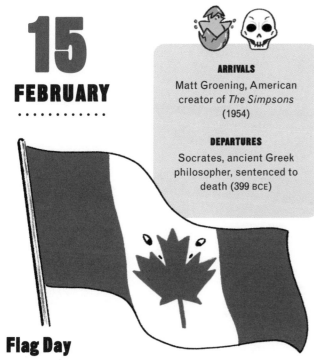

Flag Day

In 1965, the people of Canada adopt a new national flag. It has a red maple leaf on a white background with red bands. The image is striking, but some see the points of the leaf forming an image in white of two people in profile, heads touching, having an argument. What do you see?

Ready, Teddy, Go!

The first teddy bear is placed for sale in a New York shop window in 1903. It is made by sweetshop owner Morris Michtom and his wife, Rose, who call it Teddy's Bear, inspired by a newspaper cartoon showing American President Theodore "Teddy" Roosevelt sparing the life of a bear while out hunting.

16
FEBRUARY

ARRIVALS
Christopher Eccleston, British, ninth *Doctor Who* actor (1964)

DEPARTURES
Dick Bruna, Dutch *Miffy* author (2017)

Tut, Tut

In 1923, archeologist Howard Carter and his rich sponsor Lord Carnarvon open the burial chamber of the Egyptian boy pharaoh Tutankhamun, sealed for over 2,500 years. It is full of treasures, including the amazing gold coffin containing Tut's mummy. It is claimed that Lord Carnarvon's death a month later is caused by the Mummy's Curse.

TREE-MENDOUS

Today Lithuania celebrates Restoration of the State Day, a rather formal name for some fun festivities. Lithuanians dress in the red, green, and yellow of their national flag. They also enjoy sakotis, a traditional cake made horizontally on a rotating spit. Dough is drizzled on to the cake as it cooks, and the end product, placed vertically, looks like a tall iced fir tree.

17
FEBRUARY

ARRIVALS
Ed Sheeran, British singer-songwriter (1991)

DEPARTURES
Geronimo ("One Who Yawns"), Native American Apache chief (1909)

KIND OF RANDOM

This is Random Acts of Kindness Day in the USA, 24 hours to spend making others' lives a little happier. Hold a door for someone struggling, compliment a rival, tidy your room, or brush your hair without being asked. Don't worry, you can go back to normal tomorrow.

18 FEBRUARY

Over the Moon

In 1930, Elm Farm Ollie—a.k.a. Nelly J—becomes the first cow to fly in an airplane. During a 72-mile flight from Bismarck to St Louis, Missouri, USA, the Guernsey is milked, producing over 5¼ gallons of milk, which is sealed into cartons and parachuted to people below.

£5 Planet

American astronomer Clyde Tombaugh discovers a new planet in 1930. One-third the size of our moon and over 2½ billion miles away, it needs a name. A British schoolgirl called Venetia Burney suggests Pluto and wins £5 when it is picked. However, Pluto is downgraded to a dwarf planet in 2006.

ARRIVALS
John Travolta, American actor (1954)

DEPARTURES
Michelangelo, Italian artist (1564)

---

19 FEBRUARY

ARRIVALS
Jeff Kinney, American author of *Diary of a Wimpy Kid* (1971)

DEPARTURES
Karl Lagerfeld, German fashion designer (2019)

Crunch Time

Kellogg's, one of the world's best-known brands, begins in 1906 as the Battle Creek Toasted Corn Flake Company of Michigan, USA. Battle Creek was a health resort run by the Kellogg brothers, John and Will, who accidentally invented cornflakes when they overcooked some boiled wheat and then flattened it.

---

20 FEBRUARY

ARRIVALS
Cruz Beckham, British Instagram star (2005)

DEPARTURES
Clarence Nash, American voice actor and original voice of Donald Duck (1985)

Kick Off

The English Premier League is formed in 1992, a major moment in soccer history. Thanks to TV, it is now the most watched sports league in the world. Manchester United have won the championship most often, though Leicester City were unlikely champions in 2015–16, with odds of 5,000 to 1 against them.

Cat Calls

Popular opera *The Barber of Seville*, with music by Italian composer Gioachino Rossini, opens disastrously in Rome in 1816. The lead singer has a nosebleed, the audience jeers, and a stray cat wanders onstage. However, after its second performance it is hailed as a masterpiece.

21 FEBRUARY

Way to Go

Jeanne Calment is born in the city of Arles, France, in 1875. She will become the world's oldest known living human, keeping going until August 4th, 1997, reaching the age of 122 years and 164 days. Part of this she puts down to a diet rich in olive oil.

Stage Fright

Robert Coates dies in London in 1848, with history remembering him as the world's worst actor. Coates invents his own lines and wears garish homemade costumes. While appearing as Romeo in *Romeo and Juliet* his too-tight trousers split wide open, much to the delight of the audience. His Romeo also dies—twice.

22 FEBRUARY

Sheepish

Dolly the sheep, the world's first successfully cloned adult animal, is revealed by scientists in Scotland in 1997. Dolly had been produced artificially in a laboratory, rather than by breeding between a ewe and a ram. Originally codenamed 6LL3, she was named after country singer Dolly Parton.

23 FEBRUARY

Anyone for Sphairistike?

In 1874, British Major Walter Clopton Wingfield patents a game that he invented at a Christmas party in Wales just months earlier. He gives it a crazy name—sphairistike—which is bad Greek for "the art of playing ball." Played with rackets, a net, and rubber balls, the game is a hit and, thankfully, is soon renamed lawn tennis.

FINGER TIP

Today is the national day of Brunei, a tiny nation on the island of Borneo in Southeast Asia. The country's wealth comes from oil, and its ruler, the sultan, lives in the world's largest palace, with 1,788 rooms. In Brunei, it is rude to point with your forefinger. Use your right thumb instead!

24
FEBRUARY

SWEET DREAMS

Dragobete, named after a popular character in folklore, is celebrated today in Romania. Dragobete is the guardian of love, and on this day birds—and humans—choose their partners. Boys and girls gather flowers together, and if you sleep with the herb basil under your pillow, you will see your beloved in your dreams.

CHIP IN

Today is National Tortilla Chip Day in the USA. Though they seem Mexican, the chips were invented in the 1940s by Rebecca Webb Carranza, who ran a factory in Los Angeles making floury tortilla breads. She cut misshapen tortillas into triangles and deep-fried them for her family. The chips were a hit!

ARRIVALS
Wilhelm Grimm, youngest of Germany's Brothers Grimm fairy-tale writers (1786)

DEPARTURES
Henry Cavendish, British chemist who discovered hydrogen (1810)

25
FEBRUARY

ARRIVALS
George Harrison, British Beatles musician (1943)

DEPARTURES
Christopher Wren, British architect of St Paul's Cathedral, London (1723)

FILL HER UP!

Today is the national day of Kuwait, a small oil-producing nation of the Arabian Peninsula. Most of the country is flat, sandy desert, and natural water is in short supply, with rainy days a rarity. Because of this, Kuwait is one of a handful of countries in the world where bottled water is more expensive than petrol.

26
FEBRUARY

ARRIVALS
Levi Strauss, American denim jeans inventor (1829)

DEPARTURES
Jef Raskin, American Apple Macintosh computer pioneer (2005)

Take a Hike

In 1919, the Grand Canyon in Arizona, USA, becomes a national park, preserving it for future generations. The 277-mile-long rift contains the most remote community in the United States. Supai village has roughly 200 residents and can only be reached on foot (an 8-mile hike), by mule or by helicopter.

I Can See You!

In 1935, a new way of tracking moving objects by bouncing radio waves off them is demonstrated secretly for the first time by British inventor Robert Watson-Watt. An aircraft flying above a radio mast is picked up on a screen, enabling it to be detected even in darkness. RADAR—RAdio Detection And Ranging—is born.

27
FEBRUARY

ARRIVALS
Jonathan Ive, British iPod, iPad and iPhone designer (1967)

DEPARTURES
Spike Milligan, British-Irish comic and children's poet (2002)

GIVE US A HUG

Today is International Polar Bear Day, founded by the charity Polar Bears International to raise awareness of the danger posed to these wonderful white bears by the warming of their Arctic homes. Everyone is encouraged to cut their carbon emissions by lowering their heating or not driving. Do it for the bears!

28
FEBRUARY

ARRIVALS
John Tenniel, British illustrator of the first *Alice in Wonderland* (1820)

DEPARTURES
Cuauhtémoc, the last South American Aztec emperor (1525)

Mystery Music

In 1928, Russian inventor Léon Theremin patents one of the world's first electronic instruments. Named after him, the Theremin consists of two metal aerials attached to circuitry that produces a weird, eerie sound when the player waves their hands in the air—a sound used in many scary movies.

A TOAST TO ANDALUSIA!

Say "Hola!" to Andalusia Day, celebrated by this southernmost region of Spain with music, flamenco dancing, and green and white bunting—the colors of its flag. On the last school day before the holiday, children are served a free traditional breakfast: a piece of toast rubbed with garlic and sprinkled with olive oil. Bueno!

29
FEBRUARY

LOOK BEFORE YOU LEAP

Today is Leap Year Day, an extra day inserted into the calendar because of the rather inconvenient fact that the Earth takes 365.242189 days to orbit the sun, not a neat 365 days. Invented by Roman general Julius Caesar, leap years happen almost every four years, but not quite. The next leap years will be 2024, 2028, and 2032.

ARRIVALS
Gioachino Rossini, Italian composer (1792) (see February 20th)

DEPARTURES
Louise Rennison, British *Confessions of Georgia Nicolson* children's author (2016)

King Arthur

The world's first cat video star died this day in 1976, aged 16. Arthur, a short-haired white cat, appeared in over 300 cat food ads on British TV, charming viewers by scooping food out of a tin with his left paw. In fact, Arthur became so famous, the cat food ended up named after him.

MARCH

01 MARCH

Cheer Rio!

The city of Rio de Janeiro in Brazil is founded by Portuguese settlers in 1565. Rio is famous for bossa nova and samba music, its annual colorful Carnival, and the golden beaches of Copacabana and Ipanema. Here footvolley was created in 1965, a version of volleyball played with your feet.

ARRIVALS
Justin Bieber, American pop star (1994)

DEPARTURES
Paula Fox, American children's author (2017)

FUNNY BUNNY

This is St David's Day in Wales, marking the day on which the patron saint died in 589 CE. People wear leeks and daffodils on their clothes and eat traditional Welsh rabbit. Despite the name, this is a mustardy form of cheese on toast.

ITCHY AND SCRATCHY

In old English folklore, this is the day that fleas return to people's houses after the cold of winter, supposedly sweeping along the streets in a black army. Households open their doors and windows and brush out dust and dirt, in a form of spring-cleaning.

YIPEE!

The inhabitants of Yap State celebrate Yap Day today. Yap is one of the tiny islands of Micronesia north of Australia, and its people gather for a day of traditional events including colorful group dances with bamboo sticks, competitive basket weaving, and also coconut husking.

02 MARCH

Great Ape!

Monster movie *King Kong* premieres in New York in 1933 to rave reviews. It tells the story of a giant ape captured by hunters and taken to New York City, where Kong escapes and climbs the Empire State Building, taking a terrified woman with him. Kong's bloodcurdling bellows were created from recordings of real lion and tiger roars played backwards slowly.

ARRIVALS
Dr Seuss (real name Theodor Seuss Giesel), American children's author and artist (1904)

DEPARTURES
Howard Carter, British archeologist and discoverer of Tutankhamun's tomb (1939)

29

03
MARCH

WILD ABOUT NATURE

Since 2013, the United Nations have designated this World Wildlife Day. The day celebrates all the world's living things and also highlights the illegal trade in many endangered plants and animals. These include the pangolin, a nocturnal scaly anteater. Millions are stolen from the wild for use in traditional medicine.

ARRIVALS
Alexander Graham Bell, Scottish-American telephone inventor (1847) (see March 7th)

DEPARTURES
Hergé (real name Georges Remi), Belgian cartoonist and *Tintin* creator (1983)

IN THE PINK

Today is Hinamatsuri in Japan, a holiday also known as Doll's Day or Girl's Day. Young girls display small dolls dressed in historical costumes on special platforms draped with red cloth, placing a tiny emperor and empress at the top. Pink peach blossom is also added.

04
MARCH

ARRIVALS
Dav Pilkey, American illustrator and *Captain Underpants* author (1966)

DEPARTURES
Gary Gygax, American *Dungeons & Dragons* game co-creator (2008)

I GIVE YOU MY HEART

Today Lithuania celebrates St Casimir's Day with a huge market in the capital city, Vilnius. Thousands come to buy traditional foods, including heart-shaped iced gingerbreads known as Casimir's Hearts, to give to their loved ones. Also on sale are verbos—colorful arrangements of dyed wildflowers tied to sticks.

05
MARCH

ARRIVALS
Matt Lucas, British comic actor (1974)

DEPARTURES
Alessandro Volta, Italian battery inventor (1827)

First Flight

K5054, the prototype of the iconic British fighter plane the Supermarine Spitfire, takes to the skies for the first time in 1936. Famous for its role in the Battle of Britain, the plane flies for just eight minutes, but its pilot is so impressed with its looks and performance that on landing he declares: "I don't want anything touched!"

JUMP TO IT!

The small Pacific Islands nation of Vanuatu celebrates Custom Chiefs' Day, recognizing the importance of local village chieftains, known as jifs. Vanuatu claims to have invented bungee jumping. It is a traditional annual ritual for men and boys to throw themselves off 66-foot-high towers with vines tied to their ankles.

06
MARCH

ARRIVALS
Valentina Tereshkova, Russian cosmonaut and the first woman in space (1937) (see June 16th)

DEPARTURES
Louisa May Alcott, American *Little Women* author (1888)

FREEZE A JOLLY GOOD FELLOW

This is National Frozen Food Day, marking the date in 1930 when the world's first frozen food—spinach—went on sale at a grocery store in Springfield, Massachusetts, USA. The frosty greens are the brainchild of Clarence Birdseye, who had seen how native Canadian Inuit people preserved food by freezing it speedily in extremely cold weather.

Enter the Dragon

The Indonesian government creates the Komodo National Park in 1980 as a safe haven for the endangered Komodo dragon, the world's largest lizard. The dragons grow up to 10-foot long and stalk large prey such as deer and water buffalo. However, they will also hunt humans, including visiting tourists.

07
MARCH

Rings a Bell

Today in 1876, Scottish-born American inventor Alexander Graham Bell patents his new invention, the telephone. Bell's interest in sound is inspired by his mother's deafness. Just three days after lodging the patent, he makes the first ever phone call, to his laboratory assistant in another room: "Mr Watson, come here. I want to see you."

ARRIVALS
Piet Mondrian, Dutch artist (1872)

DEPARTURES
Aristotle, Greek ancient philosopher (322 BCE)

08
MARCH

WONDER WOMEN

This is International Women's Day, celebrated since 1911. Around the world, people mark the achievements of women and girls. In some countries, it is a public holiday, gifts are given to mothers and grandmothers, and the color purple is proudly worn. In other countries, it is a day of protest to call for women's equality in life with men.

ARRIVALS
Kenneth Grahame, British *The Wind in the Willows* author (1859)

DEPARTURES
Ferdinand von Zeppelin, German airship inventor (1917)

Star Quality

In 1960, work begins on building Hollywood's Walk of Fame, which runs along Hollywood Boulevard in California, USA. The first of the large pink five-pointed stars is laid the following month, dedicated to film director Stanley Kramer. Today the walk has over 2,500 stars, including the animated actors Mickey Mouse, Snoopy, and Kermit the Frog.

09
MARCH
· · · · · · ·

Lip Service

In 1562, the Italian city of Naples bans kissing in public. Anyone caught puckering up to their partner faces punishment by death. The ban is brought in to try and control the spread of plague, though the disease was actually transmitted through bites from infected fleas. Who would want to kiss one of those?

Living Doll

The first Barbie doll is launched at an American toy fair in 1959. The doll—full name Barbara Millicent Roberts—proves instantly popular despite her unlikely figure. She is launched as a fashion model but goes on to have many careers, including astronaut, computer engineer, rapper, McDonald's cashier, beekeeper, and president of the USA.

ARRIVALS
Yuri Gagarin, Russian cosmonaut and the first man in space (1934)

DEPARTURES
Mary Anning, British fossil finder (1847)

10
MARCH
· · · · · · ·

FREEDOM FIGHTER

Today is Harriet Tubman Day in the USA, in honor of the anti-slavery activist who fought on behalf of the Union Army in the American Civil War of the 1860s and helped to lead many of her fellow African Americans to freedom. This earned her the nickname "Moses."

Barking Mad

The first Crufts Dog Show is held in London in 1886, organized by a manager of a dog biscuit company. The first show has 600 entries, compared to the 25,000 or more dogs that compete today. The winner of Best in Show in 2019 is a papillon toy dog with the pedigree name of Planet Waves Forever Young Daydream Believers—Dylan for short.

Remote Possibility

The Galápagos Islands are discovered accidentally by Fray Tomás de Berlanga, Spanish-born bishop of Panama, while sailing to Peru in 1535. The bishop thinks the rocky islands are "worthless," yet, three hundred years later, British naturalist Charles Darwin finds that their unique wildlife, including giant tortoises and marine iguanas, inspires his theory of evolution (see February 12th).

ARRIVALS
Spencer Gore, British tennis player and first Wimbledon champion (1850)

DEPARTURES
Harriet Tubman, American anti-slavery activist (1913)

11 MARCH

ARRIVALS
Douglas Adams, British comic science fiction author (1952)

DEPARTURES
Philo Farnsworth, American electronic TV inventor (1971)

Paper Tiger

In the year 105 CE, Chinese inventor Cai Lun shows Emperor He of the Han dynasty some small samples of a revolutionary new material, made from a pressed and dried mixture of pulverized bark, leaves, rags, and old fishing nets. Cai Lun has created paper—without which this book would not be possible.

CORE VALUES

Many states in the USA celebrate Johnny Appleseed Day today. Appleseed (real name John Chapman) was an early American gardener who walked barefoot around the nation planting apple orchards. He lived a simple life, respected all animals, and is seen as a pioneer of nature conservation. However, it is also said that he often wore a cooking pot for a hat.

12 MARCH

ARRIVALS
Carl Hiaasen, American children's author of *Hoot* (1953)

DEPARTURES
Terry Pratchett, British author (2015)

Ballet-Hoo!

In 1832, a new ballet, *La Sylphide*, opens at the Paris Opera House. The choreographer's daughter Marie Taglioni dances the lead role. To show off her skill at dancing on the tips of her toes (*en pointe*), Marie's outfit has a very short, billowing skirt—the first tutu.

GONE BUT NOT FORGOTTEN

Today the Indian Ocean island of Mauritius celebrates its independence. The country's coat of arms features a dodo—a large flightless bird that became extinct 350 years ago. Unafraid of humans, the dodo proved an easy meal for sailors landing on the island, but lives on in the phrase "as dead as a dodo."

13 MARCH

ARRIVALS
Cori "Coco" Gauff, American rising tennis star (2004)

DEPARTURES
Robert C. Baker, American inventor of the chicken nugget (2006)

BIG ISSUE

Thailand celebrates Chang Thai Day, or National Elephant Day. Elephants have figured in Thai culture for centuries, though they are now endangered in the wild. So-called white elephants—actually a pinkish-gray—belonged to the king and could be given as unwelcome gifts, because looking after them required huge effort and crippling expense.

14
MARCH

ARRIVALS
Albert Einstein, German-American physicist (1879)

DEPARTURES
Stephen Hawking, British physicist and author (2018)

FULL CIRCLE

Maths fans know this as Pi Day, a celebration of the ratio of the circumference of a circle to its diameter. Pi (π) has a rough value of 3.14, hence the fuss on the 14th day of the third month. Computers have calculated pi to trillions of decimal places. The current world master of memorizing pi is Indian brainiac Suresh Sharma, who can recite more than 70,000 digits.

15
MARCH

ARRIVALS
Will.i.am (real name William Adams), American rapper and musician (1975)

DEPARTURES
Julius Caesar, Roman general who was stabbed to death (44 BCE)

FLYING SAUCER-Y

Back in 1953, an organization calling itself the International Flying Saucer Bureau declared March 15th to be World Contact Day. This is the one day each year when so-called ufologists around the world try and make telepathic contact with the extraterrestrial occupants of alien spaceships and have them visit us. Why not try it?

CUBE ROOT

Hungarians celebrate Nemzeti ünnep—their annual national day. The country's flag is raised outside the parliament building in the capital, Budapest, and citizens wear rosettes made from red, white, and green ribbons. Hungary is also the origin of another colorful item—the perpetually perplexing Rubik's Cube, invented by local architect and professor Ernő Rubik.

16
MARCH

Kick Off

The first FA (Football Association) Cup Final is held in 1872—the oldest soccer competition in the world. The match between Wanderers and Royal Engineers is played at a London cricket ground. It ends in a 1–0 victory for Wanderers, despite Royal Engineers employing the new tactic of passing the ball.

ARRIVALS
Caroline Herschel, German pioneering astronomer (1750)

DEPARTURES
Sergeant Stubby, American regimental mascot and the most decorated dog of the First World War (1926)

17
MARCH

GREEN SCENE

St Patrick's Day is celebrated in Ireland and by people with Irish ancestry everywhere, making it the world's most popular national festival. Little is known about the life of the enslaved person who became the Irish patron saint over 1,500 years ago, but modern festivities include parades, wearing green clothes, and even dyeing rivers bright green.

At a Stretch

British inventor Stephen Perry patents the rubber band in 1845. Bands are made by slicing tubes of rubber into thin rings. The record for the world's largest rubber band ball belongs to Joel Waul of Florida, USA, who spent four years combining 700,000 rubber bands to create a 6½-foot-wide monster nicknamed "Megaton" in 2008.

ARRIVALS
John Boyega, British *Star Wars* actor (1992)

DEPARTURES
Irène Joliot-Curie, French Nobel Prize-winning scientist (1956)

18
MARCH

SECONDHAND CLOTHES

This is Global Recycling Day, an attempt to get people to think about waste as a valuable resource to be reused rather than polluting the planet. Plastic packaging can be turned into everything from clothes to garden furniture. Amazingly, it takes just 25 soft-drink bottles to make a fleecy top.

ARRIVALS
Rudolf Diesel, German engine inventor (1858)

DEPARTURES
Chuck Berry, American rock 'n' roll pioneer (2017)

19
MARCH

ÇA VA?

ÇA VA!

ARRIVALS
Petr Mitrichev, Russian champion computer coder (1985)

DEPARTURES
Edgar Rice Burroughs, American *Tarzan* creator (1950)

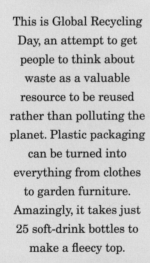

BONJOUR!

This is International Francophonie Day, when French speakers celebrate the language. Over 300 million people speak French worldwide, making it the fifth biggest language after Mandarin Chinese, English, Spanish, and Arabic. However, many non-French words have been creeping in, including *blog, wifi, burger, weekend,* and *chewing-gum.*

20 MARCH

Dog Detective

The FIFA soccer World Cup trophy is stolen from a London stamp exhibition in 1966, the thieves demanding £15,000 for its return. Instead, the trophy is found abandoned under a hedge a week later by a collie dog called Pickles, who became a celebrity. In 1983, the trophy is stolen again—in Brazil—and has never been seen since.

GOING CHEEP

This is World Sparrow Day, a celebration of the little brown birds once common in our towns and cities. Sparrow numbers are sadly falling as people remove trees and hedges and block up holes where the birds build their nests. However, humans can help by putting up special nest boxes where sparrow families can live noisily side by side.

ARRIVALS
Louis Sachar, American *Wayside School* and *Holes* author (1954)

DEPARTURES
Lev Yashin, legendary Russian soccer goalkeeper known as the "Black Spider" (1990)

---

21 MARCH

ARRIVALS
Ronaldinho, Brazilian soccer superstar (1980)

DEPARTURES
Reverend W. Awdry, British *Thomas the Tank Engine* author (1997)

TREE-MENDOUS

The United Nations celebrates both the International Day of Forests, marking their vital role in Earth's ecosystems, and World Poetry Day, in recognition of this wonderful wordy art form. The two come together in the poem "Trees" by Joyce Kilmer, which begins:
"I think that I shall never see
A poem lovely as a tree."

---

22 MARCH

ARRIVALS
Andrew Lloyd Webber, British musical theatre composer (1948)

DEPARTURES
Nicolas Flamel, French alchemist said to have discovered the philosopher's stone, as mentioned in the *Harry Potter* series (1418)

Film Premiere

The first ever screening of a motion picture takes place in Paris in 1895, with an audience of 200 people. The black-and-white film was shot by Louis Lumière and his brother Auguste, and showed workers leaving their photographic factory. It is silent, lasts just 46 seconds, and nowadays you can watch it on the internet!

23 MARCH

HUNGRY?

This is Melba Toast Day, a crispy, thin bread snack named after Dame Nellie Melba (real name Helen Porter Mitchell), a famous Australian opera singer. The toast was created for Dame Nellie in 1897 by renowned French chef Auguste Escoffier, who also invented the dessert Peach Melba in her honor.

NOBEL WOMAN

This is Pakistan Day, celebrated as a national holiday in the South Asian republic. Pakistan is home to the world's youngest ever Nobel Prize winner—Malala Yousafzai—who jointly won the Peace prize in 2014, aged just 17. Malala fights for the right of all children to have an education, and even has an asteroid named after her!

ARRIVALS
Mo Farah, British Olympic gold medal-winning track athlete (1983)

DEPARTURES
Raoul Dufy, French painter (1953)

24 MARCH

ARRIVALS
Harry Houdini (real name Ehrich Weiss), Hungarian-American magician and world's most famous escape artist (1874)

DEPARTURES
Queen Elizabeth I, British monarch (1603)

Big Bang

A new comet was spotted in 1993 by American husband and wife astronomers Eugene and Carolyn Shoemaker and Canadian fellow astronomer David Levy. The comet—named Shoemaker-Levy 9—was found orbiting the planet Jupiter and crashed into it a year later with an impact said to be 600 times greater than the world's entire nuclear arsenal.

25 MARCH

ARRIVALS
Elton John (real name Reginald Dwight), British pop star (1947)

DEPARTURES
Brian Trubshaw, first British Concorde pilot (2001)

ALL GREEK TO ME

Today Greek people celebrate their independence with a national holiday. Schools close so children can take part in parades, many of them dressed in traditional costumes and carrying the Greek flag. Hungry Greeks also tuck in to bakaliaros (salt cod fritters) and skordalia, a delicious dip made from mashed potato and garlic.

26 MARCH

EASY TIGER!

The people of Bangladesh today mark their independence with a nationwide holiday. The South Asian country's national animal is the Bengal tiger, which features on their coins and banknotes. One of the biggest of the big cats, the tiger has a roar that can be heard 2 miles away, and scary canine teeth 4 inches long!

ARRIVALS
Larry Page, American Google co-founder (1973)

DEPARTURES
Ludwig van Beethoven, German composer (1827)

PURPLE REIGN

This is Purple Day, founded in 2008 by eight-year-old Canadian Cassidy Megan, a young sufferer of the medical condition known as epilepsy. People wear purple to raise awareness of epilepsy, which causes seizures, and Cassidy's campaign is now celebrated in over 100 countries across the world!

---

27 MARCH

ARRIVALS
Wilhelm Röntgen, German X-ray discoverer (1845) (see January 5th)

DEPARTURES
Yuri Gagarin, Russian cosmonaut and first man in space (1968)

It's a Tie

The modern shoelace—complete with aglet, the little tube at each end of a shoelace that stops it from fraying—is patented by British inventor Harvey Kennedy in 1790. The current world record for most shoelaces tied in a bow in one minute is 31. Could you beat it?

Big Feet

In 2017, scientists reveal that they have found the world's largest known dinosaur footprints. The 130-million-year-old tracks of 21 different types of dinosaur were discovered in a region of Western Australia, including the 5½-foot-long prints of a giant Diplodocus-like herbivore.

---

28 MARCH

ARRIVALS
Lady Gaga (real name Stefani Germanotta), American singer (1986)

DEPARTURES
Marc Chagall, Russian-French modern artist (1985)

Plane Sailing

Hydravion, the first successful seaplane—an aircraft capable of taking off from and landing on water—is demonstrated in 1910. It is piloted by Frenchman Henri Fabre, who flies from a small lagoon near Marseilles in southern France. Henri lived to be 101, while *Hydravion* can still be seen in a museum at Bourget, north of Paris.

29
MARCH

Real Thing?

Popular legend has it that soft drink Coca-Cola was invented by American chemist John Pemberton in his backyard in Atlanta, Georgia, in 1886. Some also say he used a boat oar to stir his first batch. His still-secret recipe is thought to include vanilla, cinnamon, nutmeg, orange, lemon, and lime. Or does it?

30
MARCH

Top Tip

In 1858, a Jamaican-born businessman called Hymen Lipman is granted a patent in the USA for his handy new invention: a pencil with a little eraser attached at the end. Amazingly, before the invention of rubber erasers, people used to remove pencil marks from paper by rubbing them with little balls of bread. Try it!

BIG BREAKFAST

This is World Idli Day, a celebration of the steamed rice cakes popular in southern India. Looking like little white moons, idli are eaten for breakfast along with chutneys and sambar, a spicy lentil soup. The day was created by Eniyavan, a chef who holds the record for making the world's largest idli— a 273-pound super-snack.

31
MARCH

Tower Power

The Eiffel Tower in Paris opens in 1889. The iconic landmark is named after a man called Gustave Eiffel—the engineer whose company built it. At 1,063 feet high, it is the world's tallest building at the time. Seven million people now visit the tower annually, and one woman loved it so much she married it in 2007, becoming Erika La Tour Eiffel.

EH OH!

The Teletubbies—four brightly colored creatures with TV screens in their tummies—make their debut on British television in 1997. Tinky Winky (purple), Dipsy (green), Laa-Laa (yellow), and Po (red) live in their Tubbytronic Superdome in a field full of real rabbits—large ones chosen to make the techno-babies look smaller.

APRIL

01 APRIL

Pasta Joke

In a famous April Fool's Day stunt, a respected British TV news program broadcasts a story in 1957 that claims to show the Swiss spaghetti harvest, with people picking strands of pasta off spaghetti trees. Many viewers are fooled and want to know how to grow their own spaghetti!

YOU MUST BE JOKING!

Tomorrow is April Fool's Day. No, it's not! It's today! Fooled you! In a tradition dating back centuries, people prank or hoax their friends with silly tricks or crazy claims before loudly shouting "April Fool!" In the UK, the fun stops at midday, after which the person doing the pranking becomes the biggest fool of all.

ARRIVALS
Sophie Germain, French math genius (1776)

DEPARTURES
Scott Joplin, American ragtime composer (1917)

02 APRIL

ARRIVALS
Hans Christian Andersen, Danish fairy-tale author (1805)

DEPARTURES
Samuel Morse, American Morse code inventor (1872)

You're Fired!

In 1877, 14-year-old Rossa Matilda Richter is fired into a net from the barrel of a giant spring-loaded cannon at the Royal Aquarium in London, becoming the first human cannonball. Rossa has the stage name Zazel, the "Beautiful Human Cannonball," though some argue a child should not perform such a dangerous act.

03 APRIL

ARRIVALS
Jane Goodall, British chimp scientist (1934)

DEPARTURES
Jesse James, American Wild West outlaw (1882)

Sundae School

The ice-cream sundae is invented in New York by soda fountain owner Chester Platt in 1892. Platt takes some vanilla ice cream and covers it with cherry syrup and candied cherries, calling it a "Cherry Sunday" in honor of the day of its invention. He then goes on to invent both strawberry and chocolate versions.

Cell Mate

The first call on a cell phone—or mobile phone—is made in 1973. Martin Cooper, an engineer for electronics company Motorola, stands on a New York street and uses his huge phone (the size, shape, and weight of a brick) to call an engineer at a rival company to let him know Motorola have beaten them to it.

04
APRIL

EWE LOOK NICE

Today the people of the West African republic of Senegal celebrate their independence. Schools close and there are parades in the capital city, Dakar. Dakar sits on the coast, and every Sunday morning shepherds bring their flocks to the beach to wash them in the waters of the Atlantic Ocean and trim their hooves.

ARRIVALS
Maya Angelou, American poet (1928)

DEPARTURES
John Venn, British Venn diagram inventor (1923)

05
APRIL

ARRIVALS
Agnetha Fältskog, Swedish ABBA singer (1950)

DEPARTURES
Allen Ginsberg, US Beat Generation poet (1997)

Stoney Gaze

On this day in 1722, which happens to be Easter Sunday, Dutch explorer Jacob Roggeveen lands on a remote island in the Pacific Ocean—he calls it Easter Island. The native Polynesian people who had settled there centuries earlier called it Rapa Nui. They built the hundreds of mysterious stone figures called moai which still stare silently inland across the treeless landscape.

Fran-Tastic!

In 1971—45 years after Norwegian explorer Roald Amundsen planted his flag at the North Pole—a Canadian aviator called Frances Phipps becomes the Pole's first female visitor. Frances flew to the Pole in a ski plane and installed a radar beacon, before heading home and into the history books.

06
APRIL

ARRIVALS
John Ratzenberger, American actor who was the voice of Hamm in the *Toy Story* movies (1947)

DEPARTURES
Raphael, Italian artist (1520)

Let the Games Begin!

The first modern Olympic Games open in Athens, Greece, in 1896—over 1,500 years after the last ancient Greek games. Fourteen countries take part and all 241 competitors are male. Winning athletes are awarded a silver medal and an olive branch, with a copper medal and a laurel branch for those coming second.

Stick with It

The world is introduced to Post-it notes when they go on sale in America in 1980. The special glue that lets the notes stick and stick again had been invented accidentally years before, but no one knew what to do with it. Early prototypes were made using pale yellow scrap paper and the color, well, stuck.

07 APRIL

Dastardly Dick

The infamous highway robber Dick Turpin is executed in York, UK, in 1739. Though often portrayed as a romantic figure with a mask and pistol, Turpin was actually a burglar, horse thief, and murderer, and the story of his speedy escape to York on his horse Black Bess was invented for a novel a century later.

ARRIVALS
Jackie Chan, Hong Kongese martial arts movie star (1954)

DEPARTURES
P. T. Barnum, American circus owner, portrayed in the movie *The Greatest Showman* (1891)

TAKE A PEAK

Today the people of Slovenia celebrate their national flag. The flag carries a coat of arms showing Triglav, the highest mountain in Slovenia, with its three distinctive peaks. Slovenia has produced many famous mountain climbers, including the first married couple to conquer Mount Everest (1990).

08 APRIL

ARRIVALS
Vivienne Westwood, British fashion designer (1941)

DEPARTURES
Pablo Picasso, Spanish artist (1973)

CUSHTY!

This is International Romani Day, celebrating the Roma people and their ancient culture, which dates back over a thousand years. The Roma came from northern India but are now found all over the world. They have their own language, with many words entering English, including cushty (good), togs (clothes), and pal (friend).

09 APRIL

ARRIVALS
Isambard Kingdom Brunel, British engineer (1806)

DEPARTURES
Frank Lloyd Wright, American architect (1959)

ONE-HORN WONDERS

If you truly believe it, then this is National Unicorn Day, celebrating the mythical horse-like creature whose name means "one horn." The ancient Greeks—and many others—thought unicorns were real, believing the animals lived in India and that their horns healed sickness, but that only a pure maiden could catch one.

APRIL

10
APRIL

ARRIVALS
Daisy Ridley, British
Star Wars actor (1992)

DEPARTURES
Emiliano Zapata, Mexican
revolutionary (1919)

Pin It!

The safety pin is patented in 1849. The pin with a hidden point is the invention of New York engineer Walter Hunt, who needed a new idea to pay off a small debt. Soon afterwards, he sells his patent for $400 to a company that goes on to make millions in profits from it.

Best of the Bunch

Bananas go on sale for the first time in a London shop in 1633. The bendy fruits come from the island of Bermuda and are hung up in a window by shopkeeper Thomas Johnson. Johnson studied plants, and wrote of his bananas: "if you turn them up, they look like a boat."

11
APRIL

ARRIVALS
Jack Phillips, British
sailor and RMS *Titanic*
wireless officer (1887)

DEPARTURES
Eve Merriam, American
children's poet (1992)

Leap Frog

In 1997, the scientific journal *Nature* reports that Dutch scientists have, for the first time, made a frog float in the air inside a cylinder using super-strong magnets. The scientists have also levitated plants, grasshoppers, and fish—all without harm—and claim that humans would be possible too, with a big enough magnet.

Give Us a Bell

Inhabitants of the tiny South Pacific territory of Tokelau celebrate happily on this day in 1997, as the country becomes the last on Earth to get its own telephone network. Tokelau consists of three widely separated volcanic islands, each with a small population, and its first phone book is just two pages long.

12
APRIL

ARRIVALS
Oliver Postgate,
British writer and
Bagpuss co-creator
(1925)

DEPARTURES
Franklin Delano
Roosevelt, four-time
American president
(1945)

There and Back

In 1981, the American space agency NASA launches the space shuttle *Columbia* on its debut mission into orbit around Earth. The world's first reusable spacecraft, *Columbia* completed 27 missions and racked up over 125 million miles of travel before disintegrating while gliding home in 2003.

13
APRIL

Tip Top Tap

In 1808, African-American performer William Henry Lane, who appears under the stage name "Master Juba," is said to have perfected tap-dancing by combining elements from Irish jigs and African rhythms. People struggle to describe the new dance form, never having seen anything like it before!

ARRIVALS
Guy Fawkes, British Gunpowder Plot conspirator (1570)

DEPARTURES
Annie Jump Cannon, American pioneering astronomer (1941)

14
APRIL

ARRIVALS
Peter Capaldi, Scottish *Doctor Who* actor (1958)

DEPARTURES
Ludwik Zamenhof, Polish inventor of the language Esperanto (1917)

Sinking Feeling

At 11:40 p.m. (ship's time) on this night in 1912, the luxury liner RMS *Titanic*—on her maiden voyage to New York—strikes an iceberg, ripping a 295-foot-long hole in her hull. Supposedly unsinkable, the ship goes down less than three hours later.

Drive Time

The first Highway Code for road users is published in Britain in 1931. It costs a penny and has just 21 pages of rules, including "stop when meeting a flock of sheep." Pedal cyclists are advised not to "wobble about the road but ride as steadily as possible."

15
APRIL

ARRIVALS
Leonardo da Vinci, Italian inventor and *Mona Lisa* artist (1452)

DEPARTURES
Edward Smith, British RMS *Titanic* captain, and many passengers and crew (1912)

Rub It Out

In 1770, the great British chemist Joseph Priestley—the same person who discovered oxygen and invented fizzy drinks—finds that a small piece of vegetable gum is perfect for removing pencil marks from paper. Noting that you must rub the marks to remove them, he also invents the word rubber.

SUN DAY

This is celebrated as the Day of the Sun in North Korea and is a national holiday. The date is the birthday of North Korea's founder, Kim Il-sung, who died in 1994. It is said that for his 76th birthday in 1988, he received 43,000 presents.

16 APRIL

Hot Shot

In a 1922 sharp-shooting contest in North Carolina, USA, legendary riflewoman Annie Oakley smashes one hundred clay targets in a row, setting a new female record. Annie had been a sharp shooter since the age of eight, hitting coins in the air, shooting corks off bottles, and firing backwards while looking in a mirror.

ARRIVALS
Spike Milligan, British-Irish comic and children's poet (1918)

DEPARTURES
Madame Tussaud, French artist famous for waxworks (1850)

17 APRIL

Unlucky 13

In 1970, the command module of the American *Apollo 13* spacecraft hurtles towards Earth, while a watching world holds its breath. Launched on April 11, the moon mission has been aborted after an explosion on board. Cold and short of oxygen and water, the three crew members are thankfully rescued from the ocean alive.

ARRIVALS
Victoria Beckham, British fashion designer (1974)

DEPARTURES
Benjamin Franklin, American inventor of bifocal glasses and the lightning rod (1790)

18 APRIL

Only Natural

The Natural History Museum opens to the public in London in 1881. The museum is massive and today houses over 80 million items. Most famous of these is the replica skeleton of a Diplodocus dinosaur nicknamed Dippy. But there is also a blue whale skeleton named Hope and a preserved 28-foot giant squid called Archie.

ARRIVALS
David Tennant, Scottish *Doctor Who* actor (1971)

DEPARTURES
Albert Einstein, German-born genius scientist (1955)

LUNAR LIGHT SHOW

Today the African republic of Zimbabwe celebrates its independence. Victoria Falls, the world's largest waterfall, is at the border between Zimbabwe and its neighbor Zambia, and the spray from the thundering, falling water creates a constant rainbow, which at night under a full moon becomes a "moonbow."

19
APRIL
. . . . . .

Family

The Simpsons make their TV debut in a series of short animated inserts in an American comedy show in 1987. The characters were created by cartoonist Matt Groening and all named after members of his own family, apart from Bart—an anagram of "brat."

20
APRIL
. . . . . .

Bully Bunny

In 1979, American president Jimmy Carter is attacked by a large swamp rabbit while out fishing in a small boat in his home state of Georgia. The rabbit swims up to the boat, hissing and gnashing its teeth, and tries to climb aboard.

Racing Certainty

The world's first motor race is held in Paris in 1887. French aristocrat the Marquis de Dion and co-driver Georges Bouton won the 18-mile race driving a steam-powered quadricycle named after the Marquis's mum. It was an easy victory, as there were no other competitors.

21
APRIL
. . . . . .

Ashes to Ashes

The first space funeral occurs in 1997. An aircraft launches the cremated remains of 24 people into a 7-mile-high orbit around Earth. The deceased—including Gene Roddenberry, creator of the *Star Trek* TV series—circle the planet for the next five years before burning up on re-entry.

No Place Like Rome

The Italian capital city of Rome is said to have been founded on this day in 753 BCE by twin brothers Romulus and Remus. Legend says the boys were raised as babies by a she-wolf. Then, when they grew up, they argued so much about where to start their new city that Romulus killed Remus and named it after himself.

APRIL

22
APRIL

Getting the Hump
In 1995, Saudi Arabia holds the first of its now annual beauty contests for camels. Known unofficially as "Miss Camel," the competition judges camels on their eyelashes, ears, noses, and humps.

ARRIVALS
Yehudi Menuhin, American violin prodigy who plays from the age of seven with major orchestras (1916)

DEPARTURES
Richard Trevithick, British steam locomotive inventor (1833)

23
APRIL

In a Flap
In 1974, eccentric British inventor Arthur Pedrick patents his "chromatically selective cat flap"—a cat flap that allowed entry only to cats of a set color. He invented the device as he was fed up with next door's black cat, Blackie, stealing the food of his own cat, Ginger.

ARRIVALS
Prince Louis of Cambridge, British royal, fifth in line to the throne (2018)

DEPARTURES
William Shakespeare, British poet and playwright (1616)

Cracking Pace
In 1990, Dale Lyons runs the whole course of the London Marathon while carrying a dessert spoon with a fresh egg balanced on it. His time of 3 hours and 47 minutes makes him the fastest egg-and-spoon marathon runner to date.

24
APRIL

See for Miles
The Hubble Space Telescope is launched into orbit around Earth in 1990, having cost nearly $5 billion to build. Named after American astronomer Edwin Hubble, the telescope is a big digital camera, the size of a school bus. It is super-sensitive, and some claim it could detect a match burning on the moon.

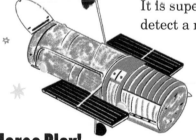

ARRIVALS
Sachin Tendulkar, Indian cricketing legend and the world's highest International scorer with over 30,000 runs (1973)

DEPARTURES
Lucy Maud Montgomery, American *Anne of Green Gables* author (1942)

Horse Play!
This is claimed to be the day in 1184 BCE when the ancient Greek army captures the city of Troy after setting siege to it for 10 years. The Greeks fool the Trojans into taking into the city a giant wooden horse with some of their soldiers hiding inside.

25 APRIL
. . . . .

ARRIVALS
Albert Uderzo,
French *Asterix* comic
illustrator (1927)

DEPARTURES
Anders Celsius,
Swedish temperature
scale inventor (1744)

Little-r Mermaid

In 1964, vandals saw off and steal the head of a bronze statue of the Little Mermaid that sits by the sea in Copenhagen, Denmark. The head of the fairy-tale figure is never recovered, so a new one is made, only for this to be sawn off in 1998. Luckily, that one is returned.

CODE BREAKERS

This is DNA Day, commemorating the date in 1953 when the world first learned the structure of the chemical that carries all the codes (genes) for replicating life. DNA (DeoxyriboNucleic Acid) is shaped like a twisted ladder. Humans have 23,000 genes, although a tiny water flea called *Daphnia* easily beats us with 31,000.

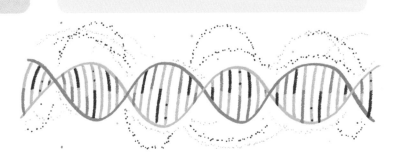

26 APRIL
. . . . . .

ARRIVALS
I. M. Pei, Chinese-
American modern
architect (1917)

DEPARTURES
Lucille Ball, American
TV comedian (1989)

ONLY HUMAN

Today is Union Day in Tanzania, celebrating the creation of the east African nation from the countries of Tanganyika and Zanzibar. The oldest known human remains, dating back almost two million years, have been found in Tanzania, from where humans then spread out across the planet.

27 APRIL
. . . . . .

ARRIVALS
Samuel Morse,
American Morse code
inventor (1791)

DEPARTURES
Ferdinand Magellan,
Portuguese explorer
(1521)

Going Ape

Koko, a female western lowland gorilla born and raised in captivity, becomes the first non-human to chat online in 1998. Taught to speak in sign language, Koko answers questions put to her by an interpreter and reveals that she likes apple juice and watching videos as well as caring for an orphaned kitten called Smokey. One of her words for bad is "toilet."

GOING DUTCH

This is Koningsdag (King's Day) in the Netherlands. People dress in orange—the color of the Royal household—a phenomenon known as "orange madness." They also sing: "Oranje boven! Oranje boven! Leve de Koning!" ("Orange on top! Orange on top! Long live the king!")

APRIL

28 APRIL

Keep off the Grass

The original Wembley Stadium in London, one of the world's most famous soccer grounds, opens in 1923, when it is home to an FA Cup final. It is built to hold 127,000 people, but about 300,000 turn up and flood the pitch—the first stadium grass ever to be called "hallowed turf."

Model Queen

The funeral of Queen Elizabeth I of England takes place at Westminster Abbey, London, in 1603, almost a month after her death. Her lead coffin has a life-size wooden effigy of her on top, dressed in royal robes, complete with crown. It can still be seen in the abbey today, along with spooky models of many other dead royals and nobles.

ARRIVALS
Oskar Schindler, German factory owner who saved many Jewish lives in the Second World War (1908)

DEPARTURES
Mary Read, British pirate who often dressed as a man (1721)

---

29 APRIL

In Other Words

In 1852, the reference book now known as *Roget's Thesaurus* is first published. Compiled by British doctor Peter Mark Roget, the book offers alternatives for specific words and proves incredibly useful, handy, helpful, beneficial, practical, and valuable to writers.

ARRIVALS
Edward "Duke" Ellington, American jazz musician (1899)

DEPARTURES
Alfred Hitchcock, British suspense film director (1980)

---

30 APRIL

Remember to Floss

Cotton candy is launched at the World's Fair in St Louis, Missouri, USA, in 1904. The machine for producing "fairy floss," as it was first called, is the invention of two men, one of whom—perhaps surprisingly—is a dentist! The British now call it candyfloss, while Greeks call it Old Lady's Hair.

ARRIVALS
Paul Jennings, British-Australian children's author (1943)

DEPARTURES
Richard Scarry, American *Busytown* children's books author and illustrator (1994)

WARM NIGHT

The German festival of Walpurgisnacht (Walpurgis Night) begins this evening and ends tomorrow. It celebrates an eighth-century saint called Walpurga, who is said to have battled witches. Huge bonfires are lit to ward off evil spirits in many European countries, including Sweden, Finland, and Czechia.

MAY

01
MAY
. . . .

MAY DAY!

This is May Day, traditionally an important spring festival in the northern half of the planet. Countries celebrate in many different ways. In Bulgaria, people jump over fires; in France, people give gifts of lily-of-the-valley; and in the town of Padstow in Cornwall, UK, a giant horse known as the Obby-Oss dances in the streets.

LEI DAY!

Since 1929, this has been Lei Day in the American island state of Hawaii. A lei is a floral garland given as a sign of welcome or affection, and each different island has its own design. Most are made of colorful blossoms, but fruits and shells also feature.

Red Card

The first ever commercial Christmas card is designed in 1843 by British artist John Callcott Horsley. The card itself is the idea of civil servant Henry Cole, who has one thousand printed to sell, though the drawing shocks some because it shows a small child drinking wine.

02
MAY
. . . .

Stray Cat Strut

In 2019, a stray cat joins the models on the catwalk during a luxury fashion show in Marrakech, Morocco. Ignoring the models, the cat walks past them in the wrong direction before leaping off the stage and spraying a spectator in the front row.

MAY-DRID

For the Spanish capital, Madrid, this is Fiesta Dos de Mayo, the day when the city celebrates victory over the occupying army of the French emperor Napoleon back in 1808. Proud *Madrileños*—as Madrid citizens call themselves—dance in the streets, and there are fireworks and parades of people in historic military costumes.

03
MAY
· · · ·

Balloonatics

In 1808, two duelists, Monsieur de Grandpré and Monsieur de Pique, face each other from hot-air balloons half a mile above Paris. Both carry blunderbusses. De Pique fires first but fails to hit his rival's balloon. De Grandpré is more successful, and De Pique's balloon crashes swiftly to the ground.

ARRIVALS
James Brown, American soul singer (1933)

DEPARTURES
Charles Fort, American researcher into strange things such as phantom cats and UFOs (1932)

Hide and Seek

The outdoor activity of geocaching is started in 2000. The first cache is stashed by American Dave Ulmer, who hides a black plastic bucket containing books, food, money, and a catapult in woods just outside Portland, Oregon, and then posts the location online. A metal plaque now marks the historic site.

04
MAY
· · · ·

Bird Brains

In 1995, a report reveals that Japanese scientists have trained pigeons to tell the difference between paintings by famous Spanish artist Pablo Picasso and famous French artist Claude Monet. It is thought the birds recognize differences in artistic style, and when asked, they peck the correct pictures.

ARRIVALS
Alice Liddell, British *Alice in Wonderland* inspiration (1852)

DEPARTURES
E. (Edith) Nesbit, British *The Railway Children* author (1924)

05
MAY
· · · ·

Top Telly

The first live TV pictures are broadcast from the summit of Mount Everest in 1988 to viewers in Japan, China, and Nepal. Mountaineers from those countries scaled the peak and are seen flying banners and scooping snow into bottles to keep as souvenirs.

ARRIVALS
Sylvia Pankhurst, British women's rights campaigner (1882)

DEPARTURES
Napoleon Bonaparte, French emperor and general (1821)

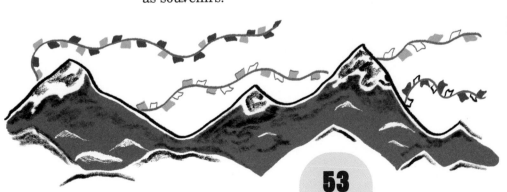

MAY

06
MAY
· · · ·

Black Day

The "penny black," the world's first adhesive postage stamp, goes into use in the UK in 1840. The stamp features a sideways portrait of the young Queen Victoria but no mention of the issuing country—and today the UK is still the only nation not to have its name on its stamps.

Run, Roger, Run!

In 1954, 25-year-old British medical student Roger Bannister becomes the first person to run a mile (1.6 kilometers) in under four minutes, clocking up a time of 3 minutes, 59.4 seconds. Bannister's record lasts just 46 days, and the men's record stands today at 3 minutes, 43 seconds.

07
MAY
· · · ·

What a Scream!

In 1994, Norway's most famous painting— *The Scream* by Edvard Munch—is recovered after having been stolen from an Oslo museum back in February. The thieves leave it in a hotel, unable to sell it because it is so famous. Another version is sold in 1995 for over $119 million.

Dig the Victory

The British Royal Navy flagship HMS *Victory* is launched in 1765. Famous as the ship on which Admiral Horatio Nelson died during the Battle of Trafalgar in 1805, *Victory* sits today in a dock in the UK naval town of Portsmouth and is the world's oldest still-working warship.

08
MAY
· · · ·

Fizz Biz Buzz

The first glass of soft drink Coca-Cola is sold at Jacobs' Pharmacy in Atlanta, Georgia, in 1886. In its first year on sale, about nine glasses of cola were drunk each day. Nowadays, people worldwide are said to down about 10,000 glasses every second.

09 MAY

Knockout Punch

The earliest known reference to a Punch and Judy show is made in 1662, when famous British diarist Samuel Pepys writes of seeing an Italian puppet play in a market square in London. Punch and Judy performers are given the honorary title of "professor."

ARRIVALS
Ferdinand Monoyer, French inventor of the lettered eye-test chart (1836)

DEPARTURES
Joseph Gay-Lussac, French chemist who discovered that water is H_2O (1850)

SOCK IT TO ME!

Of all the weird days people celebrate, this is one of the weirdest. In the USA, this is National Lost Sock Memorial Day—a time to remember all the socks that went into the wash pile but were never seen again. Lost socks, we salute you.

10 MAY

ARRIVALS
Cecila Payne-Gaposchkin, British-American astronomer who proposed that stars were mostly hydrogen and helium (1900)

DEPARTURES
Shel Silverstein, American children's author and poet (1999)

To Cap It All

The sporting cap for international matches is approved by the English Football Association in 1886. The idea has now been adopted by other countries and other sports worldwide. Early caps were handmade from velvet with satin linings and a shiny metallic tassel.

11 MAY

ARRIVALS
Salvador Dalí, Spanish surrealist artist, famous for having a pet ocelot called Babou (1904)

DEPARTURES
Bob Marley, Jamaican reggae musician (1981)

Record Book

The world's oldest known printed book, a religious text called the *Diamond Sutra*, is published in China in 868 CE. It is found in a cave over 1,000 years later and includes a picture of the Buddha preaching with a panda at his feet.

Cat's Whiskers

Mega-musical *Cats* premieres in London, UK, in 1981. Based on verses by American poet T. S. Eliot set to music by British composer Andrew Lloyd Webber, the show features humans dressed as singing and dancing pussycats and proves so popular that it runs in London for 21 years and 8,949 shows— ending on this same day in 2002.

12 MAY

RHYME TIME

Today is Limerick Day, marking the birthday in 1812 of Victorian poet Edward Lear. Here's his most famous limerick:

"There was an old man with a beard,
Who said, 'It is just as I feared!
Two owls and a hen,
Four larks and a wren,
Have all made their nests in my beard.'"

ARRIVALS
Tony Hawk, American skateboarder nicknamed "The Birdman" (1968)

DEPARTURES
Charles Barry, British "Big Ben" clock tower architect (1860)

---

13 MAY

Stick with It

The fastening tape known commercially as VELCRO is trademarked in 1958 by inventor George de Mestral. He created the name from two French words, *velour* (velvet) and *crochet* (hook), the fastener itself being inspired by hooked seeds that stuck to the fur of his dog.

Knife Story

The table knife is invented in 1637 by powerful French politician Cardinal Richelieu. At the time, dinner guests brought their own sharp, pointed knives to meals. Richelieu had the idea of providing safer knives with rounded ends. It's hard to believe we were ever without them!

ARRIVALS
Stevie Wonder, American music legend (1950)

DEPARTURES
Georges Cuvier, French naturalist who named the mastodon and the pterodactyl (1832)

---

14 MAY

Out of this World

Skylab, the USA's first space station, is launched into orbit around Earth in 1973. Its first crew joined it 11 days later, performing experiments in space for a month. While up there, the three astronauts ate special space food and had their poo and wee collected for scientists to study back on Earth.

Grease Is the Word

Skin cream Vaseline is trademarked in 1878. It was developed by Robert Chesebrough, an American chemist who found oil-rig workers were using a strange jello-like waste product called "rod-wax" to heal burns on their skin. Its brand name combines a German word for water (*Wasser*) with a Greek word for oil (*elaion*).

ARRIVALS
George Lucas, American *Star Wars* creator (1944)

DEPARTURES
Henry Heinz, American ketchup king (1919)

15 MAY
....

Fries with That?

Brothers Richard and Maurice "Mac" McDonald open the first restaurant bearing their name, in San Bernardino, California, USA, in 1940. McDonald's Bar-B-Que is a drive-in restaurant with a very simple menu: hamburger, cheeseburger, three milkshakes, fries, root beer, coffee, fizzy orange, cold milk, and cola. That's it.

Cheesy

Both Mickey and Minnie Mouse make their movie debuts in 1928 in a short, black-and-white, silent movie called *Plane Crazy* directed by Walt Disney. Mickey was inspired by a tame mouse that visited his desk at work, and was originally called Mortimer.

ARRIVALS
Frank Hornby, British Meccano inventor (1863)

DEPARTURES
Emily Dickinson, American poet (1886)

---

16 MAY
....

ARRIVALS
Olga Korbut, Belarussian Olympic gymnast, nicknamed the "Sparrow from Minsk" (1955)

DEPARTURES
Jim Henson, American *Muppets* creator and first Kermit the Frog performer (1990)

Off with Their Heads!

In 1770, 14-year-old Austrian archduchess Marie Antoinette marries Louis, the 15-year-old heir to the royal throne of France. Four years later, they become king and queen. Hated for their lavish lifestyles, both lose their heads to the guillotine in 1793, the last royals to rule France.

---

17 MAY
....

ARRIVALS
Gary Paulsen, American young adult author (1939)

DEPARTURES
John Deere, American tractor company founder (1886)

Swings and Roundabouts

In 1620, a British traveler passing through the town of Plovdiv in Bulgaria records seeing a fairground entertainment that consists of a large rotating wheel with seats on the outside in which children sit and are spun round. It is the world's first carousel or roundabout.

NOISY FOR NORWAY!

This is Norwegian Constitution Day, Norway's national day, known to Norwegians as *syttende mai* (seventeenth May). Unlike the national days of many other countries, there are no military parades. Instead, children march through towns and cities carrying flags, shouting "Hurra!" and shaking loud rattles.

18 MAY

Fairy Tail

In 1910, our planet starts to pass through the tail of Halley's Comet, as it makes another 76-year return journey close to Earth. Some warned that the world would end, and sales of telescopes and gas masks shot up. There was also a brisk trade in fake "anti-comet pills." They were not needed.

ARRIVALS
Nicholas II, last tsar of Russia (1868)

DEPARTURES
Irene Hunt, American children's author (2001)

---

19 MAY

ARRIVALS
Malcolm X, American civil rights activist (1925)

DEPARTURES
Anne Boleyn, second wife of King Henry VIII of England, beheaded (1536)

Super-Cube

The perplexing puzzle known as Rubik's Cube is invented by Hungarian architect Ernő Rubik in 1974. The toy's colorful squares can be displayed in more than 43 quintillion unique ways. It took Rubik over a month to first solve his own invention. Can you do it more quickly?

Shell Shock

In 1966, a 188-year-old tortoise called Tu'i Malila dies of natural causes. She had been a gift from the British explorer Captain James Cook to the king of Tonga in 1777 and was presented to Queen Elizabeth II when she visited the island kingdom in 1953.

---

20 MAY

ARRIVALS
R. J. (Reginald Joseph) Mitchell, British Spitfire fighter plane designer (1895)

DEPARTURES
Dame Barbara Hepworth, British sculptor (1975)

Jeans Geniuses

In 1873, tailor Jacob Davis and Levi Strauss, a cloth-seller, are jointly given an American patent for trousers made from blue denim cloth with copper rivets to strengthen the pockets. The super-strong garments, now known as jeans, were particularly popular with would-be gold-miners.

BUZZING!

Since 2017, this is World Bee Day, celebrating and thanking these invaluable insects for the work they do pollinating crops. This date was the birthday in 1734 of pioneering Slovenian beekeeper Anton Janša, who decorated his hives with colorful paintings.

21 MAY

· · · ·

Field of Dreams

In 1932, a plane piloted by American aviator Amelia Earhart lands in a field in Northern Ireland. A startled farm hand asks her: "Have you come far?" Amelia replies, "From America," having just become the first woman to fly solo across the Atlantic Ocean.

ARRIVALS
Tom Daley, British Olympic diver (1994)

DEPARTURES
Geoffrey de Havilland, British jet plane pioneer (1965)

22 MAY

· · · ·

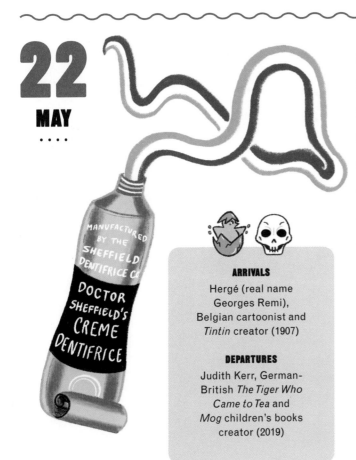

ARRIVALS
Hergé (real name Georges Remi), Belgian cartoonist and *Tintin* creator (1907)

DEPARTURES
Judith Kerr, German-British *The Tiger Who Came to Tea* and *Mog* children's books creator (2019)

Totally Tubular

Toothpaste in a tube is invented in 1892 by American dentist Washington Sheffield at the suggestion of his son Lucius, who had seen artists squeezing paint from metal tubes. The world record time for squeezing all the toothpaste from a tube with just one hand is 5.95 seconds. Don't try this at home.

Leader of the Pac

The first *Pac-Man* video game is installed in a cinema in Tokyo, Japan, in 1980. The super-hungry maze-running character was originally going to be called Puck-Man because he looked like an ice hockey puck with a piece missing. His main enemies are the ghosts Blinky, Pinky, Inky, and Clyde.

23 MAY

· · · ·

On the Hoof

The North-West Mounted Police—the forerunner of the modern Royal Canadian Mounted Police—is started in 1873. Nowadays, "Mounties" wear their distinctive red uniforms complete with riding boots and broad-brimmed hats only on ceremonial occasions. Otherwise they have gray shirts and peaked caps.

The Eyes Have It

In 1785, American inventor Benjamin Franklin announces that he has made some clever spectacles that enable him to clearly see distant objects, as well as those up close. Franklin called them "double spectacles," but they are now better known as bifocals. Older people often need them. Ask an oldie!

ARRIVALS
Ambrose Burnside, American soldier and politician whose bushy whiskers gave us the term *sideburns* (1824)

DEPARTURES
Captain William Kidd, Scottish sailor executed for piracy (1701)

MAY

24
MAY
....

ARRIVALS
Daniel Fahrenheit, Polish thermometer inventor (1686)

DEPARTURES
Nicolaus Copernicus, Polish astronomer who first proposed that Earth orbits the sun (1543)

Fangs a Lot!

The first ever World Dracula Congress, celebrating the famous fictional blood-sucking vampire, opens in Romania in 1995. In the original story by Irish author Bram Stoker, the undead Count D. lives in a castle in Transylvania, a region of Romania where people with red hair and blue eyes were once suspected of being vampires.

JUMP, BABY, JUMP!

This is the earliest day in any year on which the strange Spanish festival of El Colacho can occur. In the village of Castrillo de Murcia in northern Spain, a man dressed as the devil in a red and yellow suit jumps over a series of babies laid on mattresses in the street. He also carries giant castanets.

25
MAY
....

ARRIVALS
Igor Sikorsky, Russian helicopter pioneer (1889)

DEPARTURES
Eliza Pollock, American archer who, at 63 years and 333 days, was the oldest woman to win an Olympic gold (1919)

Hungry for Hippos?

In 1850, London Zoo takes possession of the first hippopotamus to be seen in the UK since prehistoric times. Named Obaysch after the Egyptian island where he was captured, he becomes a sensation, attracting 10,000 visitors a day and inspiring a dance called *The Hippopotamus Polka*.

Ready, Jedi, Go!

The original *Star Wars* movie introducing the characters of Luke Skywalker, Han Solo, Princess Leia, and black-clad baddie Darth Vader premieres in American cinemas in 1977. In early scripts, creator George Lucas originally intended Solo to be a green-skinned monster with gills, and Luke's surname was Starkiller.

26
MAY
....

GOING THE DISTANCE

In America, this is National Paper Airplane Day—a day to celebrate this super-simple DIY flying toy. The distance record for a paper plane is currently 226 feet 10 inches, set in 2012 by Joe Ayoob, an American football quarterback with a strong throwing arm. Can you beat it?

ARRIVALS
Sally Ride, first American woman in space (1951)

DEPARTURES
Samuel Pepys, British diarist (1703)

27
MAY
. . . .

Pig Hit

In 1933 the Walt Disney cartoon *Three Little Pigs* premieres in American cinemas. One of the most successful short movies ever, it features three musical pigs—Fifer (fife), Fiddler (violin), and Practical (piano)—trying to avoid being eaten by a hungry wolf, and makes a huge hit of the song "Who's Afraid of the Big Bad Wolf?"

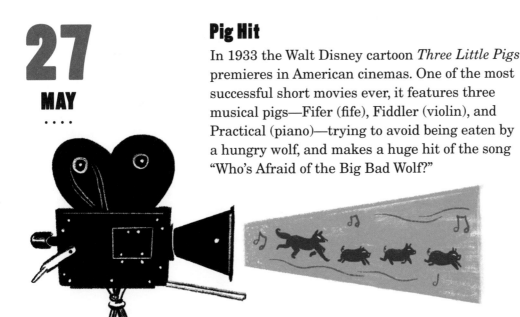

ARRIVALS
Wild Bill Hickok, American Wild West sheriff (1837), shot dead during a card game in 1876 while holding two aces and two eights, now known as the "dead man's hand"

DEPARTURES
Joseph Swan, British inventor of the light bulb (1914)

28
MAY
. . . .

ARRIVALS
Ian Fleming, British *James Bond* creator (1908)

DEPARTURES
Maya Angelou, American poet (2014)

Space Monkeys

In the USA in 1959, Able (a macaque monkey) and Miss Baker (a squirrel monkey) become the first animals to travel into space in the nose cone of a rocket and return alive. In 1984, on the 25th anniversary of her historic flight, Miss Baker is given a rubber duck and some strawberry jello as a treat.

What a Tonic!

In 1858, a new health drink is patented by Erasmus Bond of London. Its bitter taste comes from quinine, a powdered tree bark long used in India to relieve fevers. Bond blends the bitterness with other flavors to make the fizzy drink we now call tonic water.

29
MAY
. . . .

ARRIVALS
John F. Kennedy, 35th American president (1917)

DEPARTURES
Humphry Davy, British chemist who isolated several elements, including aluminum, calcium, magnesium, and sodium (1829)

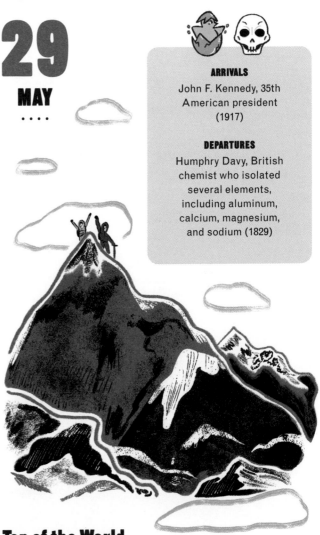

Top of the World

In 1953, New Zealand climber Edmund Hillary and Nepalese Sherpa Tenzing Norgay become the first people to stand on the summit of Mount Everest, 29,032 feet above sea level. They spend just 15 minutes there before heading down for hot soup. Today Tenzing has his very own mountain, on the dwarf planet Pluto.

30 MAY

Looking Back

The first Indy 500 motor race is held in Indianapolis, USA, in 1911. Forty cars compete, all but one driver having a mechanic sitting next to them. The exception is the eventual winner, Ray Harroun in his Marmon Wasp fitted with his new invention—the rear-view mirror—to help him see behind him.

OTTERLY LOVELY

This is World Otter Day, highlighting these playful aquatic mammals and the risks they face from hunting and habitat loss. Otters live in groups known as romps, rafts, or bevies, and use their poo, called spraint, to mark their territory. Some people claim spraint smells like jasmine tea, but not everyone agrees...

ARRIVALS
Mel Blanc, American voice actor and the original voice of Bugs Bunny (1908)

DEPARTURES
Joan of Arc, French heroine (1431)

---

31 MAY

Big Pig

The cartoon series *Peppa Pig* first airs on British TV screens in 2004. Since then, Peppa and her pals have conquered the world. One episode—"Mister Skinnylegs"—couldn't be shown in Australia because Daddy Pig tells Peppa that spiders "can't hurt you," and many spiders in Australia are highly dangerous.

ARRIVALS
Walt Whitman, American poet (1819)

DEPARTURES
Chris Haney, Canadian co-inventor of *Trivial Pursuit* board game (2010)

Pharaoh Tale

In 1279 BCE, Ramses the Second is crowned pharaoh (king) of Egypt, going on to reign for over 66 years. As king, he builds many temples and monuments adorned with giant statues of himself which still stand to this day, and his mummified remains are now on display in a museum in Cairo. Amazingly, his corpse has its own (modern) passport.

Ding Dong!

One of the world's most famous bells—Big Ben—chimes in London for the first time in 1859. Properly called the Great Bell, it is housed in the Elizabeth Tower of the Palace of Westminster and sounds an E-natural, despite developing a crack after just four months which remains to this day.

JUNE

01 JUNE
·····

ARRIVALS
Marilyn Monroe,
American movie icon
(1926)

DEPARTURES
Christopher Cockerell,
British inventor of the
hovercraft (1999)

Super, Man!

In 1938, the first issue of *Action Comics* is published in North America. The colorful cover shows a caped superhero holding a car above his head and crashing it into rocks. This is the world's first sighting of Superman, and a mint copy of that 10 cent comic book is today worth over $3 million. Super, indeed!

FAMILY TIME

Since 2012, the United Nations have declared this Global Day of Parents, a chance for children to show how much they appreciate their mums and dads. Don't worry—you don't have to buy them flowers, but you could tidy your bedroom or brush your hair.

02 JUNE
·····

ARRIVALS
Johnny Weissmuller,
Hungarian-American
Olympic swimmer and
actor who created the
"Tarzan Yell" (1904)

DEPARTURES
Peter Sallis, British
actor and voice of
Wallace in the *Wallace
and Gromit* movies (2017)

Crownpour

Queen Elizabeth II of the UK is crowned in London in 1953, having become monarch on the death of her father, King George VI, the previous year. The date is chosen because experts say it is the most reliably sunny day of the year. Sadly, it rains and everyone is soaked.

Pet Project

Europe's first Children's Zoo opens inside London Zoo in 1938. Recorded by movie news cameras, children can be seen playing with penguins, giraffes, and wallabies, being chased by ponies, and riding camels and giant tortoises. One shot even shows a seated baby stroking a wolf!

03 JUNE
·····

HIGH TIMES

This is Chimborazo Day, celebrating a snow-capped volcanic mountain in the South American nation of Ecuador. Mount Chimborazo is 20,548 feet high—not as tall as Mount Everest, but, due to the Earth bulging, Chimborazo's summit is actually the furthest point from the center of the Earth and our closest place to the moon.

ARRIVALS
Rafael Nadal, Spanish
tennis player (1986)

DEPARTURES
Muhammad Ali,
American boxer who
claimed to "Float like
a butterfly, sting like
a bee" (2016)

04
JUNE

Off Your Trolley?

The first supermarket shopping trolley is said to have been pushed into action at the Humpty Dumpty grocery store in Oklahoma, USA, in 1937. It is invented by the store's owner, Sylvan Goldman, but his idea meets resistance at first from people—mostly men—who think it is too much like pushing a pram.

05
JUNE

Chicken in a Basket

French ballooning pioneers the Montgolfier brothers demonstrate the first hot-air balloon flight using live animals before a crowd including the king and queen at the royal palace in Versailles. In the balloon's basket are a duck, a rooster, and a sheep called Montauciel—meaning "climb to the sky." All return safely to earth after an eight-minute flight.

EARTH FIRST

Since 1974, this has been World Environment Day, created by the United Nations to focus attention on all the dangers faced by the planet from climate change, pollution, and a growing human population. Tree-planting, litter-picking, and using less plastic are ways we can all help.

06
JUNE

Motion Pictures

The first drive-in movie theater opens in 1933, in New Jersey, USA. It is the idea of movie fan Richard Hollingshead, whose mum had found cinema seats uncomfortable. The first movie is a comedy called *Wife Beware*, and the event is advertised with the slogan "The whole family is welcome, no matter how noisy the children are."

HOW SWEDE

This is Sveriges Nationaldag, Sweden's national day. The Swedish royal family are presented with flowers by children in traditional costumes, and the country's distinctive blue and yellow flag is flown everywhere. Swedes also enjoy barbecues, strawberries, and homemade elderflower cordial.

JUNE

07
JUNE

Life on Mars?

In 2018, the American space agency NASA announces that its *Curiosity* rover has drilled down through rocks on the surface of Mars and found chemicals indicating that life may once have existed on the planet. However, it was probably a very long time ago. The rocks themselves are three billion years old.

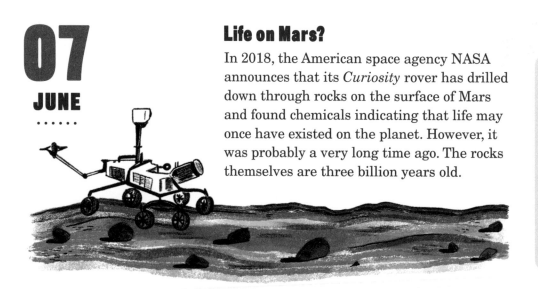

08
JUNE

Don't Bank on It

In 1987, three bank robbers try to blow open a safe inside a bank in Munkebo, Denmark, using six times the amount of explosive needed. The resulting blast can be heard over 10 miles away and demolishes the bank, but not the safe—which remains stubbornly closed.

Ball Control

The world record for the greatest distance traveled on a bike while balancing a soccer ball on your head is set in 2017 by Abdul Halim of Bangladesh. Mr Halim covers 8½ miles in 79 minutes, at times cycling one-handed while flying his national flag.

09
JUNE

REEF ENCOUNTER

Since 2012, this is Coral Triangle Day, highlighting an area of the oceans between Australia and Thailand where three quarters of the world's species of coral can be found. These amazing marine animals produce a chalky home in a wide range of bright colors and strange shapes, including some that look like human brains!

YOU MUST BE QUACKERS

Today is Donald Duck's designated birthday, being the date in 1934 when the short-tempered sailor-suited Disney character made his movie debut in a short cartoon called *The Wise Little Hen*. Donald's middle name is Fauntleroy, and, rather surprisingly, he has been criticized by some people for not wearing trousers.

10 JUNE

ARRIVALS
Maurice Sendak, American *Where the Wild Things Are* author and illustrator (1928)

DEPARTURES
Alexander the Great, Macedonian king and conqueror (323 BCE)

Roll with It

In Argentina in 1943, Hungarian refugees László and Georg Bíró patent their new invention, a pen with a tiny metal ball in the nib that rolls quick-drying ink over the paper as you write. The ballpoint pen is born and the word biro becomes shorthand for the world's most used writing instrument.

Saving Grace

In 1909 the RMS *Slavonia* sends the first Morse code SOS distress signal by radio. It consists of three short "dots," three longer "dashes," and three further "dots." The ship crashed on the coast of Portugal, but thanks to the signal all 400 passengers and crew are saved. Some claim SOS stands for "Save Our Souls," but it is simply a handy sequence.

11 JUNE

ARRIVALS
Robert Munsch, American-Canadian children's author (1945)

DEPARTURES
John Wayne, American cowboy movie actor (1979)

Great Mistake

Australia's Great Barrier Reef—the world's largest coral reef—is discovered in 1770 by British explorer Captain James Cook. Well, historians say "discovered," but actually Cook's ship, HMS *Endeavour*, hit the reef by accident and got stuck for an entire day. It was only freed by throwing lots of heavy cargo overboard.

They're Back!

Dino-packed sci-fi movie *Jurassic Park* roars into cinemas in the USA in 1993. The movie is set on a remote island where scientists have succeeded in stocking a theme park with once-extinct dinosaurs.

12 JUNE

DEAR DIARY

This is Anne Frank Day, commemorating the birthday of the brave Jewish girl who hid in a secret annex of a house in the Dutch city of Amsterdam for over two years during the Second World War, before eventually being found by the Nazis. Anne was given a diary for her 13th birthday, in which she recorded her life in hiding. This diary survived her death in 1945 and has become one of the world's most famous books.

ARRIVALS
Anne Frank, German diarist (1929)

DEPARTURES
Billy Butlin, British holiday camp king (1980)

JUNE

13
JUNE

Big Banger

In 1996, ships are alerted and bomb disposal squads scrambled to deal with what is thought to be a large explosive device floating in Hong Kong Harbor. On closer inspection, the "bomb" is declared to be an enormous seagoing sausage of unknown origin.

Victoria Line

In 1842, Queen Victoria becomes the first British monarch to travel by steam train, going from Slough, a station near her Windsor Castle home, to Paddington in central London. The journey takes 25 minutes, with the queen insisting the train never go above 30 miles per hour for fear the speed would affect her health.

ARRIVALS
European monarchs Charles the Bald (823 CE) and Charles the Fat (839 CE)

DEPARTURES
King Ludwig II, Bavarian monarch known as the "Fairy Tale King" for building grand romantic palaces (1886)

14
JUNE

Dream Music

In 1965, Beatles band member Paul McCartney records the ballad "Yesterday," which is now one of the world's best-known songs. The melody came to him in a dream and, on waking, he immediately played it on a piano to remember it. Originally, he called it "Scrambled Eggs," before composing the final lyrics.

ARRIVALS
Judith Kerr, German-British *The Tiger Who Came to Tea* and *Mog* series children's author and illustrator (1923)

DEPARTURES
John Logie Baird, Scottish inventor of television (1946)

OLD GLORY

This is Flag Day in the USA—commemorating the date in 1777 when the "Stars and Stripes" was adopted by the newly declared independent country. The first flag had just 13 stars—one for each founding state—while today there are 50, the 50th being added after Hawaii joined the union in 1959.

15
JUNE

Seal the Deal

On a small island in the River Thames in England in 1215, King John agrees to rules laid out in a legal document known today as Magna Carta (great charter). This gives rise to the joke "Where did King John sign the Magna Carta?" Answer: "At the bottom." In fact, John didn't sign his name on the document but merely attached his royal seal.

ARRIVALS
James Robertson Justice, British *Chitty Chitty Bang Bang* actor (1907)

DEPARTURES
Casey Kasem, American DJ and original voice of Shaggy in *Scooby-Doo* (2014)

16
JUNE

ARRIVALS
Jürgen Klopp, German manager of Liverpool Football Club (1967)

DEPARTURES
George Reeves, American actor and the first to play Superman on TV (1959)

Space Invader

In 1963, 26-year-old Soviet cosmonaut Valentina Tereshkova becomes the first woman in space, orbiting Earth 48 times in a tiny capsule. After almost three days, she returns safely to Earth but says her space food made her sick. She remains the youngest woman to have flown in space, and the only woman to have flown solo.

More Space Invaders!

The pioneering video game *Space Invaders* first appears in amusement arcades in Japan in 1978. Players score points by firing laser cannons at endlessly advancing rows of attacking enemy aliens modeled on octopuses, squid, and crabs. The world record for the longest continuous game remains 38 hours, 30 minutes, set by 12-year-old Canadian Eric Furrer in 1980.

17
JUNE

ARRIVALS
Venus Williams, American tennis player (1980)

DEPARTURES
Mumtaz Mahal, Mughal empress (1631)

Resting Place

Mumtaz Mahal, wife of Shah Jahan, emperor of the Mughal Empire in South Asia, dies in 1631. Her devoted husband spends the next 22 years building a beautiful white mausoleum for her as a symbol of his undying love. We know it today as the Taj Mahal in India, one of the world's most famous sights.

FIRES, NOT FRIES

This is Iceland's national day, celebrated with parades, brass bands, and riders on Icelandic horses, a breed dating back over a thousand years. Known as the "Land of Fire and Ice," Iceland has over 125 volcanic mountains and many glaciers, geysers, and hot springs, but not one branch of McDonald's.

18
JUNE

Leg-end-ary

In 1815, the Battle of Waterloo takes place in Belgium, ending in defeat for French emperor Napoleon Bonaparte. Thousands of troops die or are injured on both sides, and British military commander Lord Uxbridge loses a leg. The leg is given its own grave in a garden in Waterloo and soon becomes a major tourist attraction.

ARRIVALS
Paul McCartney, British Beatles musician (1942)

DEPARTURES
Roald Amundsen, Norwegian polar explorer and the first person to have stood at both poles (1928)

19 JUNE

Top Cat

In 2015, a Californian cat called Tara is given a National Hero Dog Award for saving her six-year-old owner from attack by an angry pooch after he fell from his bike. The brave cat sprang at the dog and drove it away. Her actions are caught on camera and get over 24 million internet views.

ARRIVALS
Nigel Gresley, Scottish designer of the world's fastest steam locomotive, *Mallard* (1876)

DEPARTURES
Koko, western lowland gorilla who communicated using sign language (2018) (see April 27th)

20 JUNE

Who's a Pretty Old Boy, Then?

Charlie, the world's oldest known budgerigar, dies in the UK in 1977. He is 29 years and 2 months old. Budgerigars are small, friendly members of the parrot family that, like parrots, can be taught to "talk." Puck—an American budgerigar who died in 1994—could mimic a record 1,728 words.

Toothy

Fishy thriller movie *Jaws*, about a marauding man-eating great white shark, is released in 1975. *Jaws* scared many moviegoers, though more people die each year from coconuts falling on their heads (about 150) than from shark attacks (about 5). In France, the film is called *Les Dents de la Mer*—"The Teeth of the Sea."

ARRIVALS
Nicole Kidman, Australian actor (1967)

DEPARTURES
Georges Lemaître, Belgian priest and astronomer who proposed the theory that the universe started with a "Big Bang" (1966)

21 JUNE

Going Bananas!

In 1997, a man called Mait Lepik wins Estonia's first banana-eating contest, wolfing 10 bendy yellow fruits in just three minutes. Instead of wasting time peeling them, Mait simply eats them whole, skins and all, winning himself an overseas holiday.

ARRIVALS
Prince William, British Duke of Cambridge (1982)

DEPARTURES
John Lee Hooker, American blues musician (2001)

HOT AND COLD

Give or take a day, this is the summer or winter solstice—the first day of summer in the northern hemisphere and the start of winter in the southern hemisphere. In the UK, hundreds of modern-day pagans gather to watch the sunrise over Stonehenge, just as its original builders did over four thousand years ago.

22
JUNE

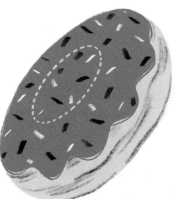

Ring of Truth?

The hole in a doughnut is supposedly invented in 1847 by a teenage American sailor called Hanson Gregory. Tired of eating deep-fried balls of dough that are still raw in the middle, Hanson cuts out the middle of a dough ball before cooking it, solving the problem. But can you invent something that isn't there?

23
JUNE

Balancing Act

In 2013, American high-wire artist Nik Wallenda becomes the first person to walk on a tightrope stretched across the Grand Canyon. The tightrope is 1,509 feet high and the walk takes almost 23 minutes, with Wallenda carrying a pole for balance. The event is broadcast live on TV with a 10-second delay in case something goes wrong.

Super-Sonic!

Sonic the speedy blue hedgehog makes his computer game debut in 1991. The creation of Japanese video game company Sega, Sonic was a squirrel, a mad-eared rabbit, and then an armadillo, possibly with fangs, before his designers settled on a hedgehog, even though the animals are not native to the USA.

24
JUNE

Match That

In 2010, American John Isner and Frenchman Nicolas Mahut play the longest tennis match in history. The first-round Men's Singles match in the Wimbledon Championships lasts 11 hours, 5 minutes and is played over three days—with Isner finally winning after 183 games.

Saucer-Eyed

In 1947, a private pilot named Kenneth Arnold spots a string of nine shiny unidentified objects flying at supersonic speed in the sky by Mount Rainier, in the US state of Washington. He describes them to the newspapers as moving like "saucers skipping on water"—and the term "flying saucer" is born.

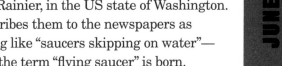

71

25 JUNE

All You Need Is a TV Set, Love

Our World, the first ever worldwide TV program, is broadcast in 1967. Thanks to a network of live satellite link-ups, the two-and-a-half-hour-long program is seen by over 400 million people in 24 countries and includes pop superstars the Beatles performing their new song "All You Need Is Love."

Wire Power

Barbed wire is patented in 1867 by American inventor Lucien Smith. Smith reckons the wire with its short metal spikes will act like an artificial thorn hedge to keep cattle contained, and be cheaper than wooden fencing. It's hard to believe, but early examples of barbed wire are highly collectible.

ARRIVALS
Eric Carle, American
The Very Hungry Caterpillar
children's author and
illustrator (1929)

DEPARTURES
George Custer,
American cavalry officer
killed at the Battle of
Little Bighorn (1876)

26 JUNE

Choose Chews

The first sale of a product using a barcode is made at a store in Troy, Ohio, USA, in 1974. The packet of Wrigley's Juicy Fruit chewing gum is bought at 8:01 a.m. by customer Clyde Dawson, and his receipt and the gum are both now on display in a major American museum.

ARRIVALS
Willy Messerschmitt,
German plane designer
(1898)

DEPARTURES
Gilbert White, British
pioneering naturalist
who had a tortoise called
Timothy (1793)

27 JUNE

Think of a Number

The world's first ATM (automated teller machine) goes into service in 1967 in the wall of a North London bank. It is invented by John Shepherd-Barron, who has the idea while lying in the bath. Originally, he proposed using a six-digit code to access money, but his wife, Caroline, could remember only four numbers, so four it was.

WAKE UP!

This is Siebenschläfertag—Seven Sleepers Day— in Germany, commemorating the ancient legend of seven youths (and a dog) who hid in a cave and nodded off for 300 years. It is claimed that the weather will stay more or less the same as today for the next seven weeks. Is it nice outside?

ARRIVALS
Tobey Maguire, American
Spider-Man movie actor
(1975)

DEPARTURES
Tove Jansson, Finnish
Moomin creator (2001)

28
JUNE

Red for Safe

In 1820, the mistaken belief that tomatoes were poisonous is finally proven wrong. For 200 years they have been cultivated as an ornament, not a food. American colonel Robert Gibbon stands on the steps of a courthouse in Salem, New Jersey, and publicly eats a whole tomato without ill effect. The pathway to the pizza is laid!

Best in Show

The world's first competitive dog show is held in 1859 in the British town of Newcastle-upon-Tyne. Only two types of dog are allowed to enter—pointers and setters—and the winners are a pointer called Bang and a setter called Dandy. Strangely, each winning dog just happens to belong to one of the judges.

29
JUNE

Hot Stuff

In 1613, the Globe, one of history's most famous theaters, is destroyed by fire. The London venue, where most of William Shakespeare's plays premiered, has its thatched roof set alight by a cannon fired during a play called *All Is True*. Luckily, no one dies. One man saves himself by pouring ale on his burning breeches.

Floss Loss

In 1994, Robert Shephard, a prisoner in a jail in South Charleston, USA, escapes by climbing up a rope he has made from braiding together 48 strands of waxed, mint-flavored dental floss bought from the jail's own shop. It no longer sells dental floss.

30
JUNE

Bridge that Gap!

Tower Bridge, over the River Thames in London, opens in 1894. The roadway of the bridge is in two parts, known as bascules, that can be lifted to let tall ships to pass underneath. In 1952, they start to open when a double-decker bus is crossing, and the driver accelerates to successfully jump a 3-foot-wide gap.

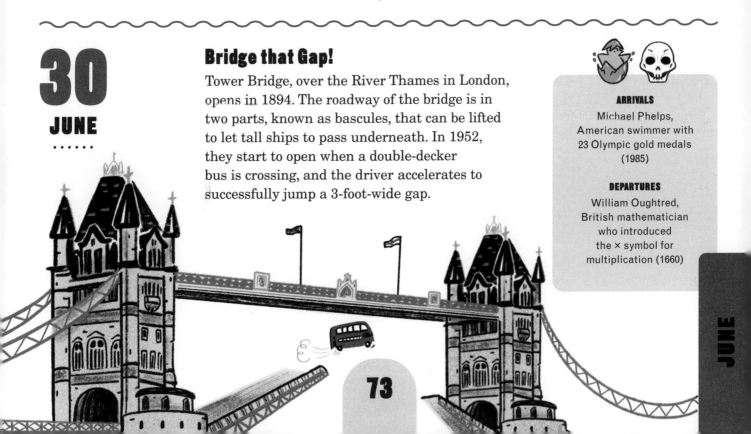

JUNE

JULY

01
JULY
· · · · ·

The Write Type

The first typewriter goes on sale in the USA in 1874. The so-called QWERTY layout—named for the first six letters in the top row of keys—is designed to make the keys less likely to jam during typing. The longest words in English that can be written with the top row only are *proprietor*, *perpetuity*, *repertoire*, and, funnily enough, *typewriter* itself.

Call Me!

The world's first emergency telephone number— 999—goes into service in central London in 1937. Chosen as it could be dialed in darkness using touch alone, the number activates a red flashing light and a siren at the telephone exchange. A week later, it helps to catch its first criminal— a burglar being chased by a homeowner.

02
JULY
· · · · ·

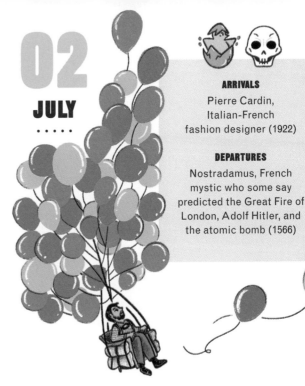

Up, Up and Away!

In 1982, a Los Angeles truck driver called Larry Walters takes to the skies by tying 45 helium-filled balloons to a garden chair. He flies for 45 minutes, rising to a height of over 14,765 feet, before using a pellet gun to burst some of the balloons and slowly return to Earth.

Up, Up and Further Away

LZ-1—the first giant airship built by German Count Ferdinand von Zeppelin—makes its maiden flight in 1900. Filled with potentially explosive hydrogen gas, the craft travels nearly four miles over a lake near the Swiss border, but it is hard to steer and sags at both ends like a sad sausage.

03
JULY
· · · · ·

No, Sir!

In 1841, the planet Neptune is discovered by British astronomer John Couch Adams. Adams was a whizz at mental math and, by observing the orbit of Uranus, simply worked out in his head where Neptune must be. He really did have "a brain the size of a planet"!

JULY

04
JULY
· · · · ·

ARRIVALS
Calvin Coolidge, 30th
American president (1872)

DEPARTURES
Marie Curie, Polish-
French scientist (1934)

Monkey Sea, Monkey Do

The tiny aquatic pets known as sea-monkeys are patented by American inventor Harold von Braunhut in 1972. They are actually tiny shrimps that live in salty water, and are sold as eggs that hatch when placed in water. Famously, sea-monkeys traveled to the moon with the *Apollo 16* and *17* lunar missions, also in 1972.

What a Liberty!

Australian hang-gliding pioneer Bill "Birdman" Bennett becomes the first person to fly a hang-glider around the Statue of Liberty in New York, in 1969. He circles the statue, soaring over the torch, before eventually landing on Liberty Island.

HOT DOG!

Today citizens of the USA celebrate its independence from Great Britain back in 1776 with fireworks, parties, and the scoffing of over 150 million hot dogs. By an odd coincidence, three American presidents have died on this day: John Adams (1826), Thomas Jefferson (also 1826), and James Monroe (1831).

05
JULY
· · · · ·

Making a Splash

The world's first bikini is revealed to the world in 1946 at a Parisian swimming pool. It is the invention of French fashion designer Louis Réard, who names the tiny garment after Bikini Atoll, an ocean island used earlier that week for an atomic bomb test.

Cook's Tour

The first ever package holiday is organized in the UK in 1841. Former preacher Thomas Cook takes five hundred people by steam train from the city of Leicester to a nearby town to hear a public talk on the dangers of drink. The day out costs just one shilling per person. Cook went on to build a huge travel empire.

ARRIVALS
Megan Rapinoe,
American women's soccer
superstar (1985)

DEPARTURES
Chester Greenwood,
American who invented
earmuffs at the age of
15 as his ears were cold
when ice-skating (1937)

06
JULY
· · · · ·

WHAT A SMACKER!

Today is International Kissing Day, a lip-smacking celebration that started in the UK in the early 2000s. The world record for the longest kiss is 58 hours, 35 minutes, 58 seconds, achieved by Thai couple Ekkachai and Laksana Tiranarat over three days in February 2013. Quick, get the lip balm!

ARRIVALS
Frida Kahlo, Mexican artist (1907)

DEPARTURES
Kenneth Grahame, British *The Wind in the Willows* author (1932)

JUMP TO IT!

Kupala Night begins tonight in the east European countries of Ukraine, Poland, Belarus, and Russia. This traditional holiday is popular with young couples, who jump over flaming bonfires while holding hands. Young women also float wreaths of flowers on lakes and rivers, with men wading in to capture them.

07
JULY
· · · · ·

ARRIVALS
Ringo Starr (real name Richard Starkey), British Beatles drummer (1940)

DEPARTURES
Arthur Conan Doyle, British *Sherlock Holmes* author (1930)

The Best Thing?

Sliced bread goes on sale for the first time in the town of Chillicothe, Missouri, USA, in 1928. Loaves—sold under the name Kleen Maid Sliced Bread—are cut and wrapped using a machine invented by former jewelry store owner Otto Rohwedder. Traditional bakeries scoff at the idea, but shoppers love the pre-cut product.

Well Done, Sun!

Solar Challenger becomes the first solar-powered aircraft to cross from France to England in 1981. Powered entirely by solar panels on the wings and stabilizers, the plane, piloted by Stephen Ptacek, takes just over five hours to travel from an airbase outside Paris to an airbase in Kent, a sunlit distance of 163 miles.

08
JULY
· · · · ·

ARRIVALS
John Pemberton, American Coca-Cola inventor (1831)

DEPARTURES
Percy Bysshe Shelley, British poet whose heart was removed after his death, then wrapped in silk and kept by his widow, Mary (1822)

Game On!

In 1969, two American inventors are granted a patent for a game played on a large mat with a grid of colorful polka dots. Uniquely, the players themselves form the playing pieces and have to bend their bodies to place feet and hands on the dots. Now known as *Twister*, the game was originally going to be called "Pretzel."

09 JULY
· · · · ·

ARRIVALS
Tom Hanks, American
Toy Story actor (1956)

DEPARTURES
King Gillette, American
inventor of the disposable
razor blade (1932)

Over the Wall

In 2005, American Danny Way becomes the first person to jump the Great Wall of China on a skateboard. Launching himself down a huge ramp from a 118-foot-tall tower, he successfully clears the more than 70-foot-wide wall despite having badly injured an ankle in an earlier unsuccessful practice jump.

Over the Wall (Again)

In 1982, at about 7 a.m., Michael Fagan scales the security wall around Buckingham Palace, the queen's private residence in London, before climbing up a drainpipe and into her bedroom. He sits on the edge of the queen's bed chatting to her before being removed by police officers.

Pussycat, Pussycat

In 1874, a large tabby cat suddenly appears during a debate in the House of Commons, the UK's famous parliamentary chamber. MPs greet the cat with loud cheers, startling it and causing it to dart forward and leap over the shoulders of several seated members, before disappearing from view.

10 JULY
· · · · ·

ARRIVALS
Arthur Ashe, American
tennis player and only
African-American man
to win three Grand Slam
titles (1943)

DEPARTURES
Mel Blanc, American voice
actor and original voice of
Bugs Bunny (1989)

On Reflection

Scottish scientist David Brewster is granted a patent for his new invention, the kaleidoscope, in 1817. Consisting of a tube containing two angled mirrors that create symmetrical reflected patterns of colored glass beads, the new toy proves so popular that 200,000 are sold in just three months.

11 JULY
· · · · ·

ARRIVALS
E. B. (Elwyn Brooks)
White, American
Charlotte's Web author
(1899)

DEPARTURES
George Gershwin,
American composer
(1937)

Feat of Clay

In 1975 it is revealed that an 8,000-strong army of life-size clay figures in the form of soldiers and horses has been unearthed by archeologists in China. Known as the Terracotta Army, they were made to guard the tomb of Emperor Qin over two thousand years ago.

12
JULY
· · · · ·

Etched into History

The drawing toy Etch A Sketch goes on sale for the first time in the USA in 1960. It is invented by Frenchman André Cassagnes, who originally called it L'Ecran Magique, "The Magic Screen." The magic is actually achieved by a stylus secretly scraping aluminum powder off a plate of glass.

Eye, Aye, Captain

Famous British admiral Horatio Nelson is blinded in his right eye in 1794 while leading troops against French forces inside the town of Calvi on the island of Corsica. Then just a captain, Nelson is hit by splinters thrown up by an explosion. He never actually wore an eye patch, as he lost his sight but not the eye.

13
JULY
· · · · ·

Unlucky 13

Austrian music composer Arnold Schoenberg dies in 1951. Despite being born on September 13th, 1874, Schoenberg had extreme triskaidekaphobia —fear of the number 13—and avoided it wherever possible. Ironically, he died at the age of 76 (7 + 6 = 13) on July 13th, 1951, which was, of course, a Friday.

14
JULY
· · · · ·

VIVE LA FRANCE!

This is Bastille Day in France, commemorating the moment in 1789 when the citizens of Paris storm the city's Bastille prison, a symbol of royal oppression. This was an early event in the French Revolution, and now the day is celebrated with parades, dancing and fireworks, and a riot of red, white, and blue everywhere.

15
JULY
· · · · ·

RAIN OR SHINE?

This is St Swithin's Day in the UK. According to folklore, whatever the weather is today, it will remain the same for the next 40 days. St Swithin was a bishop of Winchester Cathedral whose body was moved from its grave on this day in the year 971. A great storm followed by weeks of rain occurred, giving rise to the legend.

What a Spread!

In 1869, French chemist Hippolyte Mège-Mouriès patents margarine, after French emperor Napoleon III issues a challenge for someone to invent a butter-like substance that won't go off, for feeding his troops. The new spread is made from beef fat, skimmed milk, and ground cow udders. It is also pearly-white, not yellow. Nom.

ARRIVALS
Emmeline Pankhurst, British women's rights activist (1858)

DEPARTURES
Paul Gallico, American *The Snow Goose* author (1976)

16
JULY
· · · · ·

ARRIVALS
Michael Flatley, Irish creator of the dance show *Riverdance* (1958)

DEPARTURES
Anne of Cleves, fourth wife of King Henry VIII of England (1557)

Park Life

The world's first parking meter goes into operation in the American city of Oklahoma in 1935. It is invented by lawyer Carl Magee in response to complaints from local shop owners that cars stayed all day in parking spaces that customers might otherwise use. The first meters charge five cents an hour.

GREAT SNAKES!

This is World Snake Day, a global celebration of these rope-like reptiles. Fear of snakes is called ophidiophobia, the second most common phobia after the fear of spiders (arachnophobia). Snakes are actually scaly not slimy, and out of over three thousand different species only a few hundred pose any real risk to humans.

17
JULY
· · · · ·

ARRIVALS
Tom Fletcher, British musician and children's author (1985)

DEPARTURES
Billie Holiday (real name Eleanora Fagan), American jazz singer (1959)

Taking the Mickey?

Disneyland, the first Disney theme park, in Anaheim, California, opens in 1955. Things go far from smoothly: drinking fountains run dry, Main Street melts into sticky tar in the hot summer sun, Sleeping Beauty's castle almost catches fire, and the Mark Twain riverboat sinks. Disney historians still refer to it as "Black Sunday."

18
JULY
· · · · ·

ARRIVALS
Nelson Mandela, first Black South African president (1918)

DEPARTURES
Jane Austen, British novelist (1817)

Ten out of Ten

In 1976, Nadia Comăneci becomes the first ever gymnast to be awarded a perfect score of 10.0 at the Summer Olympic Games, in Montreal, Canada. The petite Romanian then achieves six more perfect 10.0s in more events, before flying home with three gold medals, two silvers, and a bronze. She is just 14 years old.

On the Fiddle

The Great Fire of Rome starts in the year 64 CE. It begins near the Circus Maximus chariot-racing stadium and burns for nine days, destroying two thirds of the city. Legend claims mad emperor Nero played the fiddle while watching the inferno—but the violin won't be invented for another 1,500 years.

19
JULY
· · · · ·

ARRIVALS
Brian May, British rock band Queen guitarist and astrophysicist (1947)

DEPARTURES
Bert Trautmann, German soccer goalkeeper who famously helped Manchester City win the 1956 FA Cup Final despite having a broken neck (2013)

Comet Tale

In 1862, American astronomer Horace Tuttle spots a new comet, the same one seen a few days earlier by fellow American stargazer Lewis Swift. Now known as Comet Swift-Tuttle, it returns slightly closer to Earth every 133 years. There is a one-in-one-million chance of it hitting Earth in the year 4479. Try not to panic.

20
JULY
· · · · ·

No Pain, No Gain

In 1976, Japanese gymnast Shun Fujimoto helps his team win gold at the Summer Olympic Games despite breaking his knee in a floor exercise. He scores 9.5 on the pommel horse and 9.7 on the rings, before dismounting perfectly to the floor and then collapsing in agony. Asked later if he would do it again, Shun replies, "No."

ARRIVALS
Sir Edmund Hillary, New Zealand mountaineer who was the first person to scale Mt Everest, along with Tenzing Norgay (1919)

DEPARTURES
Guglielmo Marconi, Italian inventor of radio (1937)

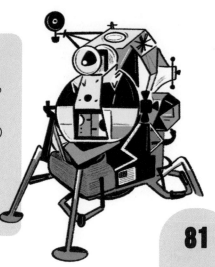

Bold Eagle

In 1969, the *Apollo 11* lunar module—named *Eagle*—touches down on the moon at precisely 20:17:40 (Coordinated Universal Time), crewed by American astronauts Edwin "Buzz" Aldrin (pilot) and Neil Armstrong (commander). Armstrong announces the moment with the historic phrase "The *Eagle* has landed." For the first time ever, man is on the moon.

21 JULY

Cold Medal

The lowest temperature ever recorded on Earth at ground level is registered in 1983 at the Vostok Station in icy Antarctica—a super-frosty figure of −128.5 degrees Fahrenheit. Scientists working there are in danger of freezing their throats when inhaling. It's also cold enough to freeze petrol.

Two Firsts

This is the day in 1969 when American astronaut Neil Armstrong becomes the first human to set foot on the moon. At exactly 02:56:15 (Coordinated Universal Time), Armstrong steps on to the powdery lunar surface with the words "That's one small step for a man, one giant leap for mankind." Buzz Aldrin follows him 19 minutes later, his first words being "Beautiful view." Just before leaving, Aldrin becomes the first human to urinate on the moon. (But don't worry, he weed inside his suit really!)

22 JULY

WHAT A RAT!

This is Ratcatcher's Day, the day in 1376 when—according to a famous poem—the mythical Pied Piper led all the children out of the German town of Hamelin, never to be seen again. The Pied Piper exacts this revenge after not being paid as promised for ridding the town of rats. Today, the real town still has both children and rats.

PI EYED

This is also Pi Approximation day. Pi—known in maths by the symbol π— is the ratio of the circumference of a circle to its diameter. Pi has been calculated to many decimal places but is roughly 3.14— the figure you get by dividing 22 (today's date) by 7 (the number of the month). Pi fans bake pies to celebrate.

23
JULY

Lick That!

The ice-cream cone is invented in 1904 at a fair in St Louis, Missouri, USA—possibly. There are other claims, but it seems that Arnold Fornachou, a Syrian ice-cream seller, ran short of paper cups and bought some hot waffles from another stallholder, which he then rolled into cones and let cool before filling them with ice cream.

24
JULY

Gran View from There

In 1987, American mountaineer Hulda Crooks becomes the oldest woman to scale Japan's highest mountain, Mount Fuji. She is 91 and wears a silk jacket with the slogan "Grandma Challenges Mount Fuji." At the summit she apparently asks, "Hey, dudes, how do I get down from here?"

Lost No Longer

Machu Picchu—often called the "lost city of the Incas"—is discovered by a historian called Hiram Bingham in the mountains of Peru in 1911. The stone ruins were once a giant estate built by the Inca people over five hundred years ago. Why they were abandoned in 1572 remains a mystery to this day.

25
JULY

Weld Done, You!

In 1984, Soviet cosmonaut Svetlana Savitskaya ventures out of the *Salyut 7* space station, orbiting 155 miles above Earth, to become the first woman to walk in space. She then spends over three and a half hours cutting and welding metal—also becoming the first human to weld in space.

Face Off

In 1976, NASA's *Viking 1* satellite takes a black-and-white photograph seeming to show a giant human-like "face" on the surface of the planet Mars. Some claim it as evidence of intelligent life on the Red Planet, but in fact the "features" are simply odd shadows on a rocky outcrop. Or are they?

26 JULY

FELIĈA ESPERANTO-TAGO (HAPPY ESPERANTO DAY)

This is Esperanto Day, an international celebration of the universal language created by Ludwik L. Zamenhof, a multilingual Polish eye doctor, in 1887. Zamenhof began developing his language while still at school with the goal of encouraging peace between different nations. In English, *esperanto* means "one who hopes."

ARRIVALS
Tanni Grey-Thompson, Welsh wheelchair athlete with 11 Paralympic gold medals (1969)

DEPARTURES
Elena Cornaro Piscopia, Italian scholar and the world's first woman to be awarded a university degree (1684)

27 JULY

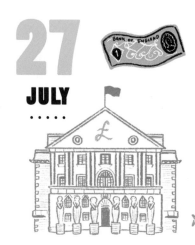

Bank on It

The Bank of England is founded in 1694. Today its vaults contain over 400,000 gold bars, worth over £200 billion (£270 billion). One gold bar, weighing 28½ pounds, is now on display in the bank's museum, where visitors can try and lift it—but you can't "borrow" it, as it's inside a special case.

ARRIVALS
Gary Gygax, American *Dungeons & Dragons* game co-creator (1938)

DEPARTURES
John Dalton, British chemist famous for his ideas about atoms (1844)

28 JULY

Hoo, What, When

One of the world's most iconic Anglo-Saxon artefacts is found in 1939. The Sutton Hoo helmet—now in the British Museum—is found in a ship burial that took place in the east of England 14 centuries ago. Reduced to fragments by time, the helmet is rebuilt like a 3D jigsaw with most of the pieces missing.

On Your Trike!

In 1883, Englishman Terah Terry becomes the first person to cross the channel between England and France on a water-tricycle—a tricycle mounted on the body of a canoe. The sea journey takes just under eight hours, but today it would be impossible as such odd vehicles are no longer allowed in French waters.

Meate and Veg

In 1586, British astronomer and mathematician Thomas Harriot returns from the new colony of Roanoke on the coast of North Carolina, USA, bearing samples of a novel new vegetable, the potato, then known by its Native American name, *openauk*. Harriot declares: "being boiled or sodden they are very good meate."

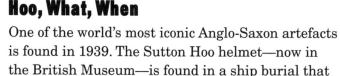

ARRIVALS
Marcel Duchamp, French-American artist who famously turned a toilet into a work of art (1887)

DEPARTURES
Johann Sebastian Bach, German composer (1750)

29
JULY

ARRIVALS
Walter Hunt, American safety pin inventor (1796) (see April 10th)

DEPARTURES
Vincent Van Gogh, Dutch artist of the *Sunflowers* (1890)

EASY, TIGER!

Wear something stripy—this is International Tiger Day, an annual celebration to raise awareness of the plight of these majestic but endangered big cats. In fact, tigers are the largest cat species on the planet. They live solitary lives in giant territories that they mark by spraying urine said to smell like buttered popcorn.

30
JULY

ARRIVALS
Emily Brontë, British *Wuthering Heights* author (1818)

DEPARTURES
Joe Shuster, Canadian-American *Superman* co-creator (1992)

Crossing the Line

In 1966, the England soccer team wins the FIFA World Cup for the first and, so far, only time. The match is played at Wembley Stadium, London, and England beats West Germany 4–2, though some claim England's third goal in extra time is invalid because the ball did not fully cross the goal line. Modern computer analysis suggests just 97 percent of the ball went over.

Roaring Success

Construction workers start building Baghdad, the capital city of Iraq, in 762 CE on the orders of ruling caliph Al-Mansur. The original city is circular, and building work begins on this date because its two main designers are also astrologers and suggest the city should have the star sign Leo.

31
JULY

Moon Racer

Forget going off-road—the first off-planet car ride takes place in 1971. *Apollo 15* astronauts David Scott and James Irwin become the first humans to drive on the moon, taking their battery-powered Lunar Roving Vehicle (aka "moon buggy") for a space-age spin, at a top speed of 8 miles per hour. It is still up there, perfectly parked.

ARRIVALS
J. K. (Joanne) Rowling, British *Harry Potter* author (1965)

DEPARTURES
Antoine de Saint-Exupéry, French *The Little Prince* author (1944)

AUGUST

01
AUGUST

ARRIVALS
Yves Saint Laurent,
French fashion designer
(1936)

DEPARTURES
Martha Jane Cannary,
American Wild West
show performer known as
"Calamity Jane" (1903)

Doggone Crazy!

In 2003 a Doberman pinscher guard dog called Barney has a moment of madness in a British tourist attraction and rips apart a display of over one hundred rare teddy bears, including one called Mabel, once owned by pop star Elvis Presley. The bears were so valuable, insurers had insisted on having a dog guard them.

SWISS CRISS-CROSS

The people of Switzerland celebrate their national day today. There are paper lantern parades and fireworks, and special cakes called "1. Augustweggen" are baked for the occasion—soft, doughy buns with a design on top resembling the distinctive square cross on the country's flag.

02
AUGUST

ARRIVALS
Elisha Gray, American
engineer who many say
invented the telephone
(1835)

DEPARTURES
Alexander Graham Bell,
British-American inventor
credited with inventing
the telephone (1922)
(see March 7th)

Hello, Yellow

Baseball history is made in 1938 in New York, USA, when a yellow—rather than white— ball is used in a major league game between the Brooklyn Dodgers and the St Louis Cardinals. Nicknamed the "stitched lemon," it is considered easier to spot, but the dye comes off on to players' hands, and a year later the yellow ball is, er, dropped.

White Sight

In 2017, a pair of rare snow-white giraffes— a mother and her calf—are filmed by wildlife rangers in the savannah of north-eastern Kenya. The giraffes are not albinos but have a condition that stops them developing the usual brown markings. Understandably, video of the tall white wonders quickly goes viral!

03
AUGUST

ARRIVALS
Elisha Otis, American inventor of the safe passenger lift (1811)

DEPARTURES
Emile Berliner, German inventor of the flat gramophone record (1929)

Fast Worker

In 1936 African-American athlete Jesse Owens famously wins the men's 100 meters dash in front of Nazi dictator Adolf Hitler at the Summer Olympic Games in Berlin, undermining Hitler's racist beliefs. A superb track and field competitor, Owens goes on to grab three more gold medals.

Ho Ho Go!

Santa Claus Land—possibly the world's first theme park—opens near the town of Santa Claus, Indiana, USA, in 1946. The park (now called Holiday World) was started by a businessman who was sad to see children turning up in the town but not finding Santa. The town also has the world's only post office named after Santa.

04
AUGUST

ARRIVALS
Barack Obama, first African-American president of the USA (1961)

DEPARTURES
Jeanne Calment, French woman who has the longest recorded human lifespan—122 years and 164 days (1997)

Bubble Trouble

Champagne is said to have been invented in 1693 by a French monk called Dom Pierre Pérignon. Legend has it that he accidentally produced a fizzy wine, which he sipped and then declared, "Come quickly! I am drinking the stars!" However, while Dom Pérignon did exist, the story is considered a lot of froth.

05
AUGUST

Fish out of Water

Tish, officially the world's oldest known goldfish, dies in 1999 at the age of 43. Tish was won at a funfair in 1956 by the son of his owner, Hilda Hand, and made the record books a year before he died. Tish is buried in a yogurt pot at the bottom of Hilda's garden in Thirsk, North Yorkshire, UK.

Man in the Water

In 1926, Hungarian-American illusionist Harry Houdini performs his last and greatest feat, spending 91 minutes inside a metal coffin submerged in a New York hotel swimming pool. The secret, he says, is controlled breathing.

ARRIVALS
Neil Armstrong, American astronaut and the first person to walk on the moon (1930)

DEPARTURES
Soichiro Honda, Japanese car company founder (1991)

06
AUGUST

ARRIVALS
Andy Warhol, American
Pop artist (1928)
(see September 25th)

DEPARTURES
John Hughes, American
Home Alone movies
creator (2009)

World Heritage Site

The world's first website goes live in 1991. Built by World Wide Web inventor Tim Berners-Lee, the page is, of course, all about his new invention, which he calls W3. There are no pictures, but you can still find the site at http://info.cern.ch/hypertext/WWW/TheProject.html.

GOING FOR GOLD

The Caribbean nation of Jamaica celebrates its independence today—unless it's a Sunday, in which case the party starts tomorrow. Jamaica is the world's only country whose flag does not contain red, white, or blue. Instead, it has a gold cross for wealth and sunshine, with black and green sections for the strong Jamaican people and their leafy island home.

07
AUGUST

ARRIVALS
Mata Hari, Dutch First
World War spy (1876)

DEPARTURES
Oliver Hardy, American
film comedian (with
partner Stan Laurel)
(1957)

In and Out

The revolving door is patented in 1888 by American inventor Theophilus Van Kannel. He claims his invention is better than a traditional door because it is noiseless and can't be blown open. However, some later speculated—without real evidence—that he invented it because he hated opening doors for other people.

Great Balls of Fire

In 1566, the people of the Swiss town of Basel experience the last of three strange celestial events. On two days in July both the sun and moon had appeared to be a different color and shape than usual, and on August 7th numerous fiery red and black balls seemed to fight a noisy high-speed battle in the sky. Were they actually early UFOs?

08
AUGUST

PURR-FECT DAY

Miaow! It's International Cat Day, founded in 2002 by an animal welfare charity. This is a day for cats to demand even more attention than they do every other day of the year. People are expected to obey their feline overlords and post yet more cute pictures and videos of cats on the internet. Is that even possible?

ARRIVALS
Jan Pienkowski, Polish-
British pop-up books
creator and *Meg and
Mog* series illustrator
(1936)

DEPARTURES
Fay Wray, Canadian-
American *King Kong*
actor (2004)

AUGUST

09
AUGUST

Mow Glee!

In 1999, American teenager Ryan Tripp—aka "Lawnmower Boy"—completes his goal of mowing the lawns of all American state capitols (buildings where the important people meet) to raise awareness of organ donation, ending outside the capitol building in Hawaii. In some states, the capitol building doesn't have a lawn, so he mowed the governor's lawn instead.

ARRIVALS
P. L. (Pamela Lyndon) Travers, Australian-British *Mary Poppins* author (1899)

DEPARTURES
Frank Whittle, British jet engine inventor (1996)

SICK NOTE

The South-East Asian nation of Singapore celebrates its independence today. Its national mascot is the merlion—a beast with a lion's head and a fish's body. In Singapore's capital, a giant merlion statue constantly shoots water from its mouth, and local doctors use the term *merlion* to refer to anyone who can't stop vomiting.

10
AUGUST

Hit and Miss

Mr Tickle, the first in the *Mr. Men* series of books by Roger Hargreaves, is published in the UK in 1971. The story is inspired by his son Adam, who wondered what a tickle looked like. To date there are over 50 different Mr Men and about 40 Little Misses, including Little Miss Stella, based on fashion designer Stella McCartney.

ARRIVALS
Tony Ross, British children's book illustrator (1938)

DEPARTURES
Rin Tin Tin, American movie-star dog originally rescued from a First World War battlefield (1932)

Smile, Please

The world-famous Louvre Museum in Paris opens to the public for the first time in 1793. Now the world's largest art museum, it houses many iconic art treasures, including the armless *Venus de Milo* statue and Leonardo da Vinci's *Mona Lisa*—a painting considered so valuable it cannot actually be insured.

11
AUGUST

Shark Ages

In 2016, scientists reveal that the slow-growing Greenland shark is probably Earth's longest-living vertebrate animal (one with a backbone). Greenland sharks grow just ⅜ inch a year, reaching a length of more than 16 feet. One female was reckoned to be at least four hundred years old—alive during the time of Shakespeare.

ARRIVALS
Enid Blyton, British children's author (1897)

DEPARTURES
Jackson Pollock, American abstract painter nicknamed "Jack the Dripper" (1956)

12
AUGUST

ARRIVALS
Ross and Norris
McWhirter, British twins
who founded *Guinness
World Records* (1925)

DEPARTURES
Cleopatra, ancient
Egyptian pharaoh
(30 BCE)

Saved Freda

In 2017, retired postman John Fletcher of Gloucester, UK, saves the life of his 45-year-old tortoise Freda by massaging her shell and giving her mouth-to-mouth resuscitation for over an hour. Freda had been drowning after accidentally falling into the garden pond, but eventually recovers enough to eat a bit of tomato and two lettuce leaves.

Bird Strike

In 1949, a large flock of starlings perches on the minute hand of Big Ben—the famous clock on the tower of London's Houses of Parliament. The sheer weight of so many birds causes the clock to slow down by almost five minutes and it is late in striking 9 p.m. Luckily, it is back to normal by midnight.

13
AUGUST

ARRIVALS
Sridevi, Indian actor
considered the "first
female superstar" of
Indian cinema (1963)

DEPARTURES
Florence Nightingale,
British nursing legend
(1910)

Soy Ahoy!

The world's first plastic car is revealed to the American public in 1941. Made by the Ford Motor Company, it has bodywork made from soy, wheat, and corn fibers mixed with hard resin instead of steel, which was in short supply due to the Second World War. Nicknamed the "Soybean Car," it runs on vegetable oil rather than petrol.

LEFT TURN

This is International Lefthanders Day, created to raise awareness about being a "southpaw," as "lefties" are also known. About 10 percent of the world's population are left-handed, with famous southpaws including Marie Curie, Oprah Winfrey, Lady Gaga, Leonardo da Vinci, Albert Einstein, and Bart Simpson.

14
AUGUST

Go, Dora, Go!

The cartoon series *Dora the Explorer* makes its debut on American television in 2000. The Latin-American character's first name was inspired by the word *exploradora*, which in Spanish means "girl scout" or "female explorer." The first Spanish word to be featured on the show is *azul* meaning "blue."

ARRIVALS
René Goscinny, French
Asterix comic writer
(1926) (see October 29th)

DEPARTURES
Enzo Ferrari, Italian
motor racing legend
(1988)

AUGUST

15
AUGUST

FAKE CHEWS

Today is Liechtenstein's national day. Residents of the tiny landlocked country are all invited to a party in the gardens of Vaduz Castle by Liechtenstein's Prince Hans-Adam II, Europe's richest monarch. The prince's wealth comes from banking, while the country itself is the world's largest manufacturer of false teeth.

ARRIVALS
Napoleon Bonaparte, French emperor and general (1769)

DEPARTURES
Macbeth, Scottish king made famous by Shakespeare (1057)

Oh, Wow!

In 1977, a signal is received by the "Big Ear" radio telescope at Ohio State University, which seems to come from an artificial, extraterrestrial source in the constellation Sagittarius. It is known as the Wow! signal because of the reaction of the astronomer who spotted it.

16
AUGUST

Gentle Giant

In 1996, a three-year-old boy falls into the gorilla enclosure at Brookfield Zoo near Chicago, USA, cutting his face and breaking his hand. The now unconscious child is then cradled gently by a female western lowland gorilla called Binti Jua, who protects him until he is rescued by a keeper. The boy later makes a full recovery.

ARRIVALS
Liz Pichon, British *Tom Gates* series children's author (1963)

DEPARTURES
Elvis Presley, American singer known as the "King of Rock 'n' Roll" (1977)

Simple Simon

The IBM Simon—the world's first smartphone, complete with antenna, apps, and a stylus—goes on sale in 1994. A big gray brick weighing in at a whole pound, the Simon is limited by a battery life of just one hour, despite costing $899 dollars—the equivalent of over $1,500 dollars today.

17
AUGUST

Clowning Around

The first ever animated movie premieres in Paris, France, in 1908. Called *Fantasmagorie*, it is hand-drawn by cartoonist Emile Cohl in a style similar to chalk drawings on a blackboard. The movie features a top-hatted man and a clown in a series of strange happenings, and lasts just 1 minute, 20 seconds.

ARRIVALS
Davy Crockett, American soldier known as "King of the Wild Frontier" (1786)

DEPARTURES
Ludwig Mies van der Rohe, German-American skyscraper architect (1969)

18
AUGUST

New World, Newborn

Virginia Dare, the first child born on American soil to British parents, enters the world in 1587. She is a member of the Roanoke Colony, a group of British settlers off the coast of what is now North Carolina who all mysteriously disappeared within just a few years. To this day, no one knows what happened to them.

Screen Time

Television is invented by Russian scientist Constantin Perskyi in 1900. Well, not the high-tech device we stare at, but the word *television* itself. He uses the word in a report written for a Paris conference on electricity—combining the Greek word *tele*, meaning "distant," with the Latin word *visio*, "sight."

tele visio...

What a Gas!

The lighter-than-air gas helium is discovered in 1868 by French astronomer Pierre Jules Janssen. Observing the sun during a total solar eclipse in India, Janssen realizes that the band of yellow light he detects is coming from an element not yet known on Earth. Helium is named after *helios*—the Greek word for "sun."

19
AUGUST

Stick with It

In 1924, Frank Epperson is granted a patent for something he had invented accidentally 19 years earlier: the Popsicle ice lolly. Aged 11, he left a glass of flavored water with a wooden stirrer in it outside his Oakland, California, home and it froze solid overnight. Epperson originally called it the "Eppsicle," but his kids renamed it the Popsicle.

CLOSE COUSINS

This is International Orangutan Day, raising awareness of these adorable apes whose homes on the South-East Asian islands of Sumatra and Borneo are being destroyed by deforestation. The name *orangutan* comes from two Malay words meaning "human of the forest"—very appropriate given they share 97 percent of our DNA.

20
AUGUST

Green Teen

In 2018, 15-year-old student Greta Thunberg skips school to stage a climate-change protest outside the Swedish parliament building in Stockholm. This is her first school strike—an idea that spreads across the world in a matter of months, and sees her named *Time* magazine's Person of the Year in 2019.

Bags for Life?

The plastic carrier bag is introduced to the world in 1960. They were invented by Swedish engineer Sten Gustaf Thulin, who thought they would be good for the planet because they would save trees from being felled to make paper bags. Little did he know…

21
AUGUST

Mona Loser

In 1911, Leonardo da Vinci's *Mona Lisa* is stolen from the Louvre Museum in Paris. It remains missing until December 1913, when it is recovered from the thief, Vincenzo Peruggia. In that time, more people visit the Louvre to see the empty space than had previously come to view the painting itself.

Slice of the Action

In 1991, a bizarre battle breaks out in the town of Independence, Missouri, USA, between two costumed characters promoting rival pizza restaurants. A man advertising Domino's Pizza while dressed in a furry red rabbit suit is knocked unconscious by Bobo the Clown from the Pizza Hut across the street.

22
AUGUST

Saints Preserve Us!

In the year 565 CE, Irish missionary St Columba is walking by the shore of Loch Ness in the Scottish Highlands when he claims to see a large beast about to attack a man swimming in the water. Columba raises his hand and commands the monster to "go back with all speed." Miraculously, it obeys him.

23 AUGUST

Frog Power

The world's largest known frog is caught in Equatorial Guinea, Africa, in 1960. The aptly named goliath frog weighs over 7 pounds, with adults often over 12 inches long.

ARRIVALS
Dick Bruna, Dutch *Miffy* author (1927)

DEPARTURES
Naum Gabo, Russian sculptor (1977)

Going My Way?

The first ever one-way streets are introduced in the City of London in 1617 in an attempt to control "the disorder and rude behavior of carmen, draymen, and others using cartes." Seventeen streets are made one way, including Pudding Lane, where the Great Fire of London will start 50 years later.

24 AUGUST

Blow Your Top

Mount Vesuvius, a volcano in Italy, begins erupting violently in 79 CE, famously destroying the town of Pompeii and its inhabitants. The eruption is witnessed by Roman historian Pliny the Younger, who describes a cloud like "a pine tree" rising from the summit. Three million nearby residents remain at risk today.

ARRIVALS
Linton Kwesi Johnson, Jamaican dub poet (1952)

DEPARTURES
Thomas Blood, Irish soldier who tried to steal the British Crown Jewels (1680)

25 AUGUST

On the Ball

RoboCup-97—the world's first soccer tournament for robots—opens in Nagoya, Japan, in 1997. Five thousand people come to see matches played between high-tech teams of self-propelled robots. The finals on August 28th see victory for American robots in the Small-Size League and Japanese success in the Middle-Size League.

ARRIVALS
King Ludwig II, Bavarian monarch known as the "Fairy Tale King" for his extravagant castles (1845)

DEPARTURES
Neil Armstrong, American astronaut and the first person to walk on the moon (2012)

In the Swim

In 1875, British sea captain Matthew Webb finally comes ashore at Calais, on the north coast of France, thereby becoming the first known person to swim the English Channel without artificial aids. He had set off from Dover, England, 21 hours, 40 minutes earlier, smeared in porpoise oil and favoring the breaststroke.

26 AUGUST

Mini, Ha Ha!

One of the world's most recognizable small cars—the Morris Mini-Minor—is revealed to the British public in 1959. At less than 10 feet long, the Mini goes on to become an icon of the 1960s and sparks a craze for seeing how many people will fit inside. The current record for a classic Mini is 27, set in 2014.

27 AUGUST

Fast Work

The first *Guinness Book of Records* is published in 1955. The book arose from a Guinness breweries boss wondering what the fastest game bird in Europe was. Unable to find out, he commissioned his own book of odd records. It is now the bestselling copyrighted book in the world. And FYI, the fastest game bird in Europe is the golden plover.

More Balloonacy

The first ever flight by a balloon filled with hydrogen gas takes place in Paris, France, in 1783. The launch attracts a huge crowd. The balloon flies north for 13 miles, before landing in the village of Gonesse. Here local peasants shoot it with a gun and attack it with pitchforks, thinking it is a monster from Hell.

28 AUGUST

Horse versus "Iron Horse"

In 1830, *Tom Thumb*, the first steam locomotive to be built in America, races against a horse-drawn passenger-car to prove its superiority—and loses. Racing on parallel tracks, the locomotive soon takes the lead, but an engine failure means only the horse completes the contest. Despite this, the days of horse-drawn power are numbered.

29
AUGUST

Dish of the Day

The Chinese takeout staple chop suey—a mix of meat, eggs, and vegetables—is possibly invented in 1896, but not in China. Legend has it that a Chinese diplomat visiting New York has his chef create an oriental-style dish that would appeal to the tastes of some American dinner guests. Other legends are available.

Ashes to Ashes

In 1882, the cricketing rivalry known as the Ashes begins. It is sparked by a joke obituary in a British sports paper after a home defeat to Australia, which claims that British cricket would be cremated "and the ashes taken to Australia." Both teams now compete for a tiny urn containing the ashes from some burned bails.

30
AUGUST

FRY-DAY

This is Amagwinya Day, a celebration of the deep-fried doughy treat popular in Botswana and South Africa, where they are commonly sold by street vendors. Amagwinya are similar to a hole-less donut, and some people eat them with savory sausage, while Botswanan schoolchildren are said to adore amagwinya and chips. Nom.

Oodles of Doodles

The first ever Google Doodle appears on the home page of the popular American search engine in 1998. It features the symbol of the Burning Man Festival, an annual American cultural event, as well as the colorful Google logo. More recent doodles have included playable *Pac-Man* games and working hip-hop DJ turntables.

31
AUGUST

HOW LOW CAN YOU GO?

Today the Caribbean nation of Trinidad and Tobago celebrates its independence with calypso music, steel drum bands, and limbo dancing, all of which originated here. Limbo dancing—bending backwards to pass under a low horizontal bar—was originally done at funerals, and the current record low is just 8½ inches.

AUGUST

SEPTEMBER

01
SEPTEMBER

Pigeon's Last Post

Martha, the world's last passenger pigeon, dies in 1914 at the Cincinnati Zoo, USA. Passenger pigeons once numbered in their billions across America, traveling in huge flocks that blocked out the sun. Hunting drove them to extinction, and the now-stuffed Martha survives as a powerful symbol for preserving nature.

Stamp's First Post

This is a red-letter day for stamp collectors. In 1853, the South African colony known as the Cape of Good Hope issues the world's first triangular postage stamps. The sticky three-sided stamps have a value of one penny (red) or four pennies (blue), but today collectors pay up to $380,000 for examples with printing errors. Lick that!

02
SEPTEMBER

London's Burning

The Great Fire of London breaks out in 1666, beginning at a bakery in Pudding Lane and spreading to destroy over 13,000 houses and the medieval St Paul's Cathedral over the course of four days. Despite the destruction, only six direct deaths are known.

Well Done, You

In 1986, American inventor Ralph R. Piro is granted a patent for a shoulder-mounted device capable of giving the wearer a self-congratulatory pat on the back using a fake hand worked by a rope. While this sounds odd, many inventors have patented similar machines for kicking oneself in the bottom.

03
SEPTEMBER

Days Gone By

Something strange happens to this day in the UK in 1752—it vanishes. The country switches from the Julian calendar (named after Julius Caesar) to the Gregorian calendar (named after Pope Gregory XIII, who introduced it in 1582). As a result, September 3rd instantly becomes September 14th and angry mobs take to the streets demanding, "Give us back our 11 days!"

04 SEPTEMBER

Rabbit On

In 1893, British author Beatrix Potter writes a letter to the young son of a friend who is recovering from illness. She includes some lovely sketches of rabbits and states, "I shall tell you a story about four little rabbits, whose names were Flopsy, Mopsy, Cottontail and Peter." The now-famous Peter Rabbit stories are born.

Data Delivery

Technology giant Google is founded in California, USA, in 1998 by university students Larry Page and Sergey Brin. Their main product, an internet search engine, is originally called "BackRub." The present name is a misspelling of *googol*—which is a very large number (the number 1 followed by 100 zeros)—chosen to reflect the huge amount of data the search engine can deliver.

ARRIVALS
Beyoncé Knowles, American pop star (1981)

DEPARTURES
Steve Irwin, Australian zookeeper known as "The Crocodile Hunter," stabbed by a stingray fish (2006)

05 SEPTEMBER

Close Shave

Russian tsar Peter the Great introduces a tax on beards in 1698, in an attempt to make the chins of Russian men look more modern. Peasants and clergymen are exempt, but anyone else with a beard has to produce a "beard token" to prove they have paid the tax, or risk being shaved on the spot.

ARRIVALS
Freddie Mercury, British Queen singer (1946)

DEPARTURES
Crazy Horse, Native American Lakota war chief (1877)

06 SEPTEMBER

Stumped?

In 1776, a cricket wicket of three stumps—rather than just two—is first used in a match between the British teams of Coulsdon and Chertsey. The middle stump is introduced after a professional cricketer known as "Lumpy" Stevens bowls three balls in succession through a two-stump wicket without the batsman being declared out.

Boldly Going

The American TV series *Star Trek* premieres (in Canada, surprisingly) in 1966. Captain James Kirk and the crew of the starship *Enterprise* are said to be on a five-year mission to explore strange new worlds, but the series is axed after just three years despite protests from fans. It is now a hugely successful movie franchise.

ARRIVALS
Buddy Bolden, American pioneering jazz musician (1877)

DEPARTURES
Arthur Rackham, British children's book illustrator (1939)

07
SEPTEMBER

Saving Grace

In the early hours of this day in 1838, Grace Darling, a British lighthouse-keeper's daughter, spots a passenger ship that has become wrecked on rocks off the coast of Northumberland. Despite the stormy seas, she and her father row over to rescue nine surviving passengers, Grace becoming a heroine in the process.

Earth Movers

In 2001, starting at exactly 11 a.m., about one million schoolchildren across the UK jump up and down for a minute to see if scientists can detect them on instruments used to measure earthquakes. Sadly, the Giant Jump doesn't register, but it does set a record for the most people jumping at once.

08
SEPTEMBER

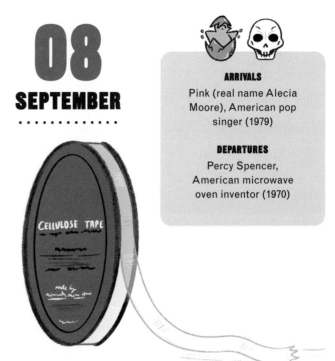

Tale of the Tape

See-through adhesive tape goes on sale for the first time in America in 1930. It is the invention of Richard Drew, an employee of the Minnesota Mining and Manufacturing Company (now known as 3M). While adhesive tape itself is safe in normal use, scientists have found that unpeeling a roll at speed in a vacuum generates X-rays!

David's Day

In 1504, in the Italian city of Florence, *David*, one of the world's most famous statues, is finally unveiled. Carved by the great Renaissance artist Michelangelo, the 17-foot-high marble figure weighs 6¼ tons, took two years to sculpt, and originally wore a well-placed golden garland.

09
SEPTEMBER

Loopy

In 1913, Russian military pilot Pyotr Nesterov becomes the first person to fly a loop, previously thought impossible. He loops-the-loop above an aerodrome outside Kiev, but is arrested immediately on landing and charged with "risking government property." However, he is later hailed a hero and given a medal.

10
SEPTEMBER

Collision Course

The Large Hadron Collider—the world's most powerful subatomic particle smasher—is activated by scientists in Geneva, Switzerland, in 2008. Also the world's largest machine, the 17-mile circular tube packed with powerful, super-cooled magnets develops a fault just nine days later and remains out of action for over a year. Oops.

Off with His Head!

In 1945 farmer Lloyd Olsen of Fruita, Colorado, USA, tries to kill a chicken named Mike with an ax. Most of Mike's head comes off, but enough remains for him to stay alive for almost two years, touring fairs and being fed with an eyedropper. Mike the Headless Chicken Day is celebrated in Fruita every May.

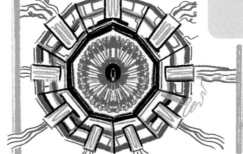

ARRIVALS
Chris Columbus, American *Home Alone* and *Harry Potter* movie director (1958)

DEPARTURES
Charles Cruft, British Crufts dog show founder (1938)

11
SEPTEMBER

Big Bennu

In 1999, American astronomers discover a 1,640-foot-wide asteroid orbiting close to Earth. Named Bennu, after a mythical bird of ancient Egypt, it is as old as our solar system. A space probe will land on it and return to Earth in 2023 with the first ever samples taken from an asteroid, possibly with clues to how life began here.

ARRIVALS
Philip Ardagh, British *Eddie Dickens* series children's author (1961)

DEPARTURES
Roger Hargreaves, British *Mr. Men* and *Little Miss* children's books author and illustrator (1988)

12
SEPTEMBER

Girl Power

In 1910, American Alice Stebbins Wells is sworn in as an officer in the Los Angeles Police Department, making her the world's first known official policewoman. She is given a rule book and a badge, but has to make her own uniform—a gold-trimmed khaki jacket with a floor-length skirt.

In the Dark

Lascaux Cave, containing some of the world's best prehistoric cave paintings, is found accidentally near Montignac, France, in 1940 by four schoolboys when their dog falls in a hole. The 17,000-year-old images depict animals including cattle, deer, ibex, the extinct ox-like aurochs, and a horned horse that some say is a unicorn.

ARRIVALS
Jesse Owens, American Olympic gold medal-winning athlete (1913) (see August 3rd)

DEPARTURES
Tom Sims, American inventor of the snowboard (2012)

102

13
SEPTEMBER

Wall Power

Roman legionaries in the north of the UK begin building Hadrian's Wall in 122 CE. Named after the emperor Hadrian—who probably designed it—the wall runs 72¾ miles across the UK and takes 15,000 men six years to finish. However, it does not mark the border between England and Scotland. That lies further north.

Scooby New

TV's most famous Great Dane dog makes his debut in 1969 with the American broadcast of "What a Night for a Knight"—the first episode of cartoon series *Scooby Doo, Where Are You!* Scooby and friends Fred, Daphne, Velma, and Shaggy solve their first mystery, investigating a Black Knight who comes alive with the full moon.

14
SEPTEMBER

Full Moon

Luna 2, a spacecraft launched by the Soviet Union, becomes the first manmade object to strike the moon, in 1959. The rocket had been launched two days earlier and hits the surface at over 6,800 miles per hour, releasing a giant cloud of gas visible from Earth and scattering lots of small metal markers—the very first lunar litter.

Muscling In

The world's first ever bodybuilding contest, the Great Competition, takes place in 1901 in London's Royal Albert Hall. Fifteen thousand people turn up to watch 60 muscly men be judged on their physique. The champion is British bodybuilder William Murray, who wins a whopping one thousand guineas (over $135,000 in today's money) and a gold statue.

15
SEPTEMBER

Evolutionary Matters

In 1835, the British expeditionary ship HMS *Beagle* arrives at the remote Galapagos Islands, off the coast of Ecuador. On board is a young naturalist called Charles Darwin, whose observations of the islands' unique wildlife—strange finches, giant tortoises, and marine iguanas—will inspire his radical ideas about evolution.

SEPTEMBER

16
SEPTEMBER

All the Way

The festive favorite "Jingle Bells" is copyrighted by its American composer, James Pierpont, in 1857, under its original title "One Horse Open Sleigh." Now popular worldwide, it becomes the first song to be broadcast from space when it is performed on December 16th, 1965, by the crew of the *Gemini VI-A* space mission.

Sinking Feeling

The first recorded hole-in-one in golf is scored in 1869 by 18-year-old Scottish professional golfer "Young" Tom Morris. Young Tom aces the shot on the 492-foot, par-three eighth hole of Prestwick Golf Club in Scotland, and his historic scorecard can still be seen in the clubhouse today.

17
SEPTEMBER

All Washed Up

In 1997, five hundred cucumbers painted five different colors are thrown into the Irish Sea in a serious study of the tidal currents between the UK and Ireland. Experts were keen to find out why so many sheep droppings were washing up on English beaches. The sheep themselves were saying nothing.

Plaque Attack

Dutch scientist Antonie van Leeuwenhoek writes a letter in 1683 to the leading scientific body in London in which he describes using his new invention, the microscope, to observe little moving "animalcules" living in the plaque on his teeth. It is the first recorded sighting of bacteria, but he clearly needs to brush more often.

18
SEPTEMBER

Thar She Blows!

In 1870, an expedition through what is now Yellowstone National Park in Wyoming, USA, comes across a geyser that spouts boiling water over 90 feet into the air nine times during the course of an afternoon. Because it's so regular, they call it "Old Faithful." The geyser is still going strong 150 years later.

19
SEPTEMBER

YO HO!

Ahoy, me hearties! This is International Talk Like a Pirate Day—created in 1995 by Americans Mark Summers (pirate name Cap'n Slappy) and John Baur (Ol' Chumbucket). Just like old-time buccaneers, the idea has now traveled far across the globe, as has the joke: Why are pirates called pirates? Because they "Arrrrr!"

Out Cold

In 1991, two German tourists come across a body frozen in the ice on the mountains between Austria and Italy. Later examination reveals it to be the remains of a man who had died around 3300 BCE. Nicknamed "Ötzi the Iceman," the corpse has 61 tattoos and his very last meal was red deer meat and bread.

20
SEPTEMBER

Serve You Right

In 1973, former American men's tennis champion Bobby Riggs plays Billie Jean King, the USA's number one women's player, in an attempt to prove that men are better at tennis. Billed as the "Battle of the Sexes," the match is played at Houston Astrodome, Texas. Ms King wins in three sets, 6–4, 6–3, 6–3.

Slice of the Action

The forerunner of the modern pizza cutter, a knife with a circular rolling blade, is patented in 1892 by David S. Morgan of North Carolina, USA. However, Morgan's invention was originally intended for cutting wallpaper. Not quite so tasty.

21
SEPTEMBER

Claus for Thought

In 1897, the New York newspaper *The Sun* carries an editorial column written in response to a letter from eight-year-old Virginia O'Hanlon asking, "Is there a Santa Claus?" The paper's reply, "Yes, Virginia, there is a Santa Claus," becomes famous worldwide and inspires books, movies, and TV shows. Virginia grows up to become a schoolteacher.

22
SEPTEMBER

FAR OUT

Today the people of the West African republic of Mali celebrate their independence. The country's capital is Bamako—which means "crocodile tail" in the local language—and the Malian city of Timbuktu, at the edge of the Sahara desert, is famous for being far away, as in the phrase "from here to Timbuktu."

MIDDLE EARTH BIRTH

Do you wear colorful clothes and have hairy feet? If you do, great news—this is Hobbit Day, a celebration of the creatures invented by British author J. R. R. Tolkien. In Tolkien's novels *The Hobbit* and *The Lord of the Rings*, today is the shared birthday of top hobbits Bilbo and Frodo Baggins, and some fans celebrate by going barefooted.

ARRIVALS
Tom Felton, British actor who played Draco Malfoy in the *Harry Potter* movies (1987)

DEPARTURES
Shaka, Zulu king in southern Africa (1828)

23
SEPTEMBER

ARRIVALS
Augustus, first Roman emperor (63 BCE)

DEPARTURES
Bob Fosse, American choreographer and film director (1987)

On the Cards

Japanese video game company Nintendo is founded in 1889 by Tokyo businessman Fusajiro Yamauchi. Almost a century before *Super Mario Bros*, Nintendo originally make *hanafuda*—colorful playing cards decorated with images of flowers such as cherry blossoms and chrysanthemums. Despite many theories, no one is quite sure what the name Nintendo actually means.

New Chew News

Chewing gum is first sold in America in 1848. Native Americans and others have long been chewing tree resin before this, but businessman John B. Curtis is the first to boil up spruce tree resin, add beeswax and flavorings, then wrap the result in paper and sell it as "State of Maine Pure Spruce Gum." Sounds delicious.

24
SEPTEMBER

ARRIVALS
Jim Henson, American *Muppets* creator and first Kermit the Frog performer (1936)

DEPARTURES
Dr Seuss (real name Theodor Geisel), American *How the Grinch Stole Christmas!* author (1991)

Rocktastic

Devils Tower in Wyoming, one of the world's most striking rock formations, becomes America's first National Monument in 1906. The 5,115-foot-high steep-sided butte features in the movie *Close Encounters of the Third Kind* and is sacred to many Native American tribes, some saying the grooves on its sides were made by giant bears.

25 SEPTEMBER

Soupy Success

An exhibition entitled "New Painting of Common Objects" opens at the Pasadena Art Museum, California, USA, in 1962. It features works by eight artists including Andy Warhol and Roy Lichtenstein, and is the first museum show of what will become known as Pop art. Warhol's contribution includes his famous soup-can prints.

ARRIVALS
Will Smith,
American actor (1968)

DEPARTURES
Johann Strauss,
Austrian waltz composer
(1849)

---

26 SEPTEMBER

ARRIVALS
Serena Williams,
American tennis player
(1981)

DEPARTURES
Levi Strauss, German-
American blue jeans
maker (1902)

Digital Fish Dish

The batter-coated fish strips known as fish fingers officially go on sale for the first time in the UK in 1955. They were invented by frozen food specialist Clarence Birdseye and nearly called Battered Cod Pieces, until his factory workers voted for Fish Fingers instead. Other countries call them fish sticks.

Eco-Warriors

In 1991, four men and four women enter a giant sealed research facility in Arizona, USA, called Biosphere 2 to try and survive only on the plants and animals also living within it. The experiment runs for two full years and is largely successful, though the human "terranauts" soon split into two bad-tempered rival groups.

---

27 SEPTEMBER

ARRIVALS
Avril Lavigne, Canadian
pop singer (1984)

DEPARTURES
Sylvia Pankhurst,
British women's rights
campaigner
(1960)

Rat Surprise

In 2017, scientists confirm the existence of the vika, a rat that was rumored to live in trees in the Solomon Islands and thought to be so big that it was capable of cracking open coconuts. An injured specimen, orange-brown and 18 inches long, is found during tree felling, which is a major threat to its continued survival.

Train of Events

In 1825, *Locomotion No. 1* becomes the first steam locomotive to haul passengers on a public railway. Built by British engineers George and Robert Stephenson, *No. 1* pulls several hundred people in open wagons between Stockton and Darlington in northern England, taking two hours to travel just 8½ miles—almost the same amount of time it would take to walk it.

28
SEPTEMBER

ASK TASK

This is Ask a Stupid Question Day, created in the 1980s by some American teachers keen to encourage students to ask questions, no matter how dumb they might seem. So, go on, ask someone "What's the speed of dark?" "Why isn't there mouse-flavored cat food?" "Is baby oil made from babies?" Go on, ask!

Long Shot

Legend has it that in 1918 Private Henry Tandey, a British soldier serving in France during the First World War, encounters an enemy German soldier but spares his life because he is injured. That lucky soldier is Lance Corporal Adolf Hitler, future leader of Nazi Germany—or so Hitler himself later claims.

29
SEPTEMBER

Is It a Bird?

In 2013, several people report seeing a strange winged figure flying between trees in a park in central Santiago, Chile, before disappearing. Witnesses describe the creature as having a human body and leathery wings like a manta ray, leading it to be nicknamed "Manta-Man." Skeptics think it was just a bird.

It Grows on You

In 2015, the American Society for Microbiology launches the first of its annual Agar Art Contests. All the entries are designs formed by growing different-colored fungi and bacteria on special jello in sealed dishes. The winning entry is a depiction of human nerve cells made from pretty orange and yellow microbes.

30
SEPTEMBER

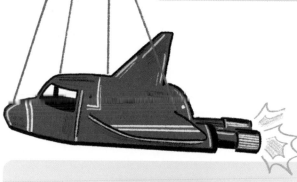

FAB SHOW

5, 4, 3, 2, 1... International Thunderbirds Day is GO! In 1965, the first ever episode of the daring puppet action series *Thunderbirds*, set in 2065, is broadcast on British TV. All five International Rescue pilots—Scott, Virgil, Alan, Gordon, and John Tracy—are named after pioneering real-life American astronauts.

OCTOBER

01
OCTOBER

Bang on Time

The super-fast Tokaido Shinkansen railway service opens in Japan in 1964. Nicknamed the "bullet train," it can travel at 130 miles per hour and operates between the capital, Tokyo, and the city of Osaka. Modern Japanese bullet trains can hit 199 miles per hour—about one eighth of the speed of an actual bullet.

T Time

The first Ford Model T motor car goes on sale in 1908. Built on an assembly line to keep it cheap, the iconic car makes motoring affordable for families. It is called the "T" because it is Ford's twentieth attempt to produce a successful design, starting from Model A. Owners affectionately call it the "Tin Lizzie."

Beeton's Winner

Mrs Beeton's Book of Household Management—one of the world's most famous cookery books—goes on sale in Britain in 1861. Written by 21-year-old Isabella Beeton, it contains two thousand recipes, as well as her opinions that garlic is "offensive," potatoes are "suspicious," and pasta should be boiled for almost two hours.

02
OCTOBER

Jog On

The first ever Parkrun takes place in Bushy Park, London, in 2004. It is organized by Paul Sinton-Hewitt, who is unable to run marathons because of a leg injury. The first 13 entrants are all his friends, invited to come for a pre-breakfast jog. Amazingly, Parkrun now has over six million members worldwide.

Good Grief!

The *Peanuts* cartoon strip, created by Charles M. Schulz, debuts in seven American newspapers in 1950. The first four-frame cartoon features loveable loser Charlie Brown (minus his zigzag-striped jumper), with super-smart beagle Snoopy appearing two days later. Despite its success, Schulz always hated the title *Peanuts*.

03
OCTOBER

Future King

In 1945, future American rock 'n' roll superstar Elvis Presley gives his first public performance when he enters a talent competition at the Mississippi-Alabama Fair and Dairy Show. The 10-year-old Elvis—destined to become the bestselling solo music artist of all time—has to stand on a chair to sing, and only comes fifth.

TWO BECOME ONE

At the stroke of midnight on this day in 1990, the countries of East and West Germany, divided for 45 years, are rejoined—an event celebrated as German Unity Day. One continuing difference is that the traffic-light man at pedestrian crossings in the former East Germany wears a straw hat and is a much-loved figure known as "Ampelmännchen."

04
OCTOBER

Up and Down Career

In 1911, the London Underground railway opens its first escalators for public use at Earl's Court station. To prove to passengers that the new-fangled moving stairways are safe to use, an engineer with a wooden leg, called "Bumper" Harris, is employed to travel up and down them all day long.

IT'S FIKA TIME!

In Sweden, this is a day to really sink your teeth into. It's Kanelbullens dag—Cinnamon Bun Day—a celebration of the sticky pastry treat, flavored with spices and topped with white icing. The buns are commonly enjoyed with friends during *fika*—a traditional Swedish coffee break.

05
OCTOBER

Splashing Out

The world's first costume specifically designed for sea bathing is said to have gone on sale in 1830 at Farley's, a clothing store in Baker Street, London. The garment is made of muslin, wool, and linen, though why anyone might want to buy a bathing costume in chilly October remains a mystery.

OCTOBER

06
OCTOBER

UTTER MADNESS

This is Mad Hatter Day, in honor of the Hatter from children's classic *Alice in Wonderland*. In the original illustrations to the book, the Mad Hatter is pictured at a perpetual tea-party in a huge top hat with a price tag reading "10/6" (ten shillings and sixpence)—hence the date chosen for the celebration. In real life, hat makers were often affected by the chemicals they used, hence the phrase "as mad as a hatter."

ARRIVALS
Lonnie Johnson, American inventor of the Super Soaker water gun (1949)

DEPARTURES
Will Keith Kellogg, American co-inventor of cornflakes (1951) (see February 19th)

07
OCTOBER

Far and Near

The far side of the moon is photographed for the first time in 1959 by Soviet Russian space probe *Luna 3*, revealing it to be quite like the side that always faces us here on Earth. Mistakenly called the "dark side," the far side gets as much sunlight each month as the near side: two weeks' worth.

ARRIVALS
Simon Cowell, British TV personality and music producer (1959)

DEPARTURES
Clarence Birdseye, American frozen food pioneer (1956)

On the Slide

In 2000, Slovenian daredevil Davo Karničar becomes the first person to ski down to base camp from the summit of Mount Everest. The 11,810-foot descent takes the skier 4 hours, 40 minutes to complete and is live-streamed to four million viewers worldwide, though the historic video has sadly since been lost.

08
OCTOBER

Ting! Thing

In 1945, American electronics company Raytheon files a patent for the microwave oven. The heating properties of invisible microwave radiation had been discovered accidentally by employee Percy Spencer, who found microwaves melted a chocolate bar in his pocket. Popcorn was the first food to be microwaved on purpose.

ARRIVALS
R. L. (Robert Lawrence) Stine, American *Goosebumps* children's author (1943)

DEPARTURES
Felix Salten, Austrian *Bambi* author (1945)

09
OCTOBER

Flying Low

In 1890, French aviation pioneer Clément Ader flies a steam-powered airplane for roughly 160 feet across the grounds of a chateau in northern France. His flying machine, the *Éole*, has bat-like wings and gains a height of about 8 inches, but cannot be steered, unlike the Wright brothers' *Flyer I* of 1903 (see December 17th).

Car Crash

In 1992, 18-year-old Michelle Knapp of Peekskill, New York, USA, hears a loud bang while watching TV and runs outside to find that a rock about the size of a bowling ball has hit her parked car and traveled straight through, making a hole in the ground below. The rock is warm to the touch and smells of rotten eggs, and is in fact a meteorite from space. Luckily, all is not lost. She later sells both the rock and her wrecked car to collectors.

10
OCTOBER

Stroke of Genius

In 1989, American inventor Rita Della Vecchia patents a "Scratching and Petting Device for Household Pets." Rita's petter consists of a jointed, wall-mounted arm with a model hand on the end of it. A dog or cat in need of some love simply triggers an electronic sensor, and the arm extends to pet it on demand.

11
OCTOBER

MERRY MICHAELMAS!

In Britain, this is Old Michaelmas Day. Folklore says that on this day the devil fell out of heaven and landed in a blackberry bush, the prickly briar making him so cross that he spat and stamped on the fruit. As a result, superstitious people still reckon this is the last day in the year on which blackberries should be picked.

OCTOBER

12
OCTOBER

Prost!

The giant German beer festival known as Oktoberfest is held for the first time in 1810. The Bavarian city of Munich organizes the fair to celebrate a recent royal wedding, ending with a horse race. Two hundred years later, Oktoberfest now starts in September because the weather is better, and in 1896, a young Albert Einstein helped set up one of the beer tents.

ARRIVALS
August Horch, German founder of Audi car brand (1868)

DEPARTURES
Grape-kun, Humboldt penguin who famously "fell in love" with a cut-out of a cartoon penguin in a Japanese zoo (2017)

13
OCTOBER

Thank You, Mr Bond

Paddington, the accident-prone bear from "darkest Peru," makes his debut in 1958, with the publication of the book *A Bear Called Paddington*. The creation of British TV cameraman Michael Bond, Paddington was inspired by a teddy bear Bond saw sitting all alone on a toy department shelf one Christmas Eve. He bought the bear as a gift for his wife.

Lady's First

In 1908, British women's rights campaigner Margaret Travers Symons becomes the first woman to speak in the British House of Commons. While on a tour of the Houses of Parliament, she bursts into the chamber during an (all-male) debate and shouts, "Votes for women!"

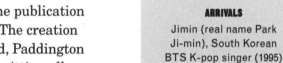

ARRIVALS
Jimin (real name Park Ji-min), South Korean BTS K-pop singer (1995)

DEPARTURES
E. C. (Elzie Crisler) Segar, American cartoonist and creator of Popeye (1938)

14
OCTOBER

Night Light

The world's first ever floodlit soccer match is played at Bramall Lane, Sheffield, UK, in 1878. A huge crowd turns up to watch an evening game between teams known simply as the Reds and the Blues, lit by four electric lamps at the corners of the pitch. Despite players being frequently blinded by the lights, the Blues win 2–0.

ARRIVALS
Ralph Lauren, American fashion designer (1939)

DEPARTURES
King Harold II, English monarch killed at the Battle of Hastings (1066)

15 OCTOBER

Crunch Time

The pillow-shaped breakfast cereal known as Shredded Wheat is patented in 1895. The wheaty treat was invented by American vegetarian Henry Perky, who was looking for a food that might help relieve his runny tummy. Unusually for a popular breakfast cereal, shredded wheat has no added salt or sugar.

You Will!

In 1839, British Queen Victoria sends for her German cousin Prince Albert and asks him to marry her. Albert, of course, agrees and they are married within four months. Victoria wears a white wedding dress rather than royal robes, starting a fashion for white that is still going today.

16 OCTOBER

Royal Hedwig

In 1384, Jadwiga is crowned Poland's new king—an unusual achievement for a 10-year-old *girl*. The German form of the name Jadwiga is Hedwig, shared with Harry Potter's snowy owl. Although the character is female, in the movies Hedwig is played by a male owl. Or rather, eight different ones: Gizmo, Ook, Sprout, Kaspar, Swoops, Oh Oh, Elmo, and Bandit.

Here's One I Made Earlier

Blue Peter, the world's longest-running children's TV show, starts today in 1958. It is famous for pets, crafts, and the catchphrase, "Here's one I made earlier." Viewers receive badges for special achievements, a gold badge being the highest honor. Recipients include Queen Elizabeth II, David Attenborough, and assistance dog Endal, a Labrador retriever who could use a cash machine.

17 OCTOBER

Cruel Blow

London was hit by a powerful tornado in 1091, the first recorded in British history. Savage winds demolished an entire church, 600 wooden houses, and the newly-built London Bridge over the River Thames. The rebuild was then destroyed by fire 40 years later, possibly inspiring the nursery rhyme, "London Bridge is Falling Down."

18
OCTOBER
. . . .

ARRIVALS
Martina Navratilova,
Czech-American tennis
legend (1956)

DEPARTURES
Thomas Edison,
American inventor (1931)

Art Failure

In 1961, the prestigious New York Museum of Modern Art goofs and hangs a paper-cut artwork called *Le Bateau* (The Boat) by famous French artist Henri Matisse upside down. The mistake isn't noticed for six weeks.

Space Cat

Félicette becomes the first cat in space in 1963. The black and white cat, with monitors attached, is fired into space in the nose cone of a French rocket. Her 15-minute flight includes a brief period of weightlessness and her capsule returns safely to Earth by parachute, earning her the nickname "Astrocat."

19
OCTOBER
. . . .

ARRIVALS
Philip Pullman, British
His Dark Materials
author (1946)

DEPARTURES
Jonathan Swift, Irish
Gulliver's Travels author
(1745) (see October 28th)

Get the Message?

In 2017, astronomer Robert Weryk spots a strange dark red object tumbling through space. Possibly cigar-shaped and about 20 million miles from Earth, it is given the Hawaiian name 'Oumuamua, meaning "first distant messenger." 'Oumuamua is the only object known to come from outside our solar system, and is probably a fragment of a distant planet, rather than an alien spaceship.

Unboxing

In 2003, American illusionist David Blaine finally emerges from a clear plastic box in which he had been suspended—without food—beside the River Thames in London for 44 days, in a stunt called "Above the Below." Blaine declares, "I love you all!", before being rushed to hospital, having lost a quarter of his body weight.

20
OCTOBER
. . . .

Big Deal?

In 1967, two American filmmakers, Roger Patterson and Bob Gimlin, visit a remote forested spot in northern California and shoot about a minute of footage showing a large, hairy ape-like creature walking upright by a river. Plaster casts of its footprints are nearly 16 inches long. Nicknamed "Bigfoot," is the beast real or a hoax?

ARRIVALS
Kamala Harris, high-
profile Asian-American
politician and first
female vice president of
the United States (1964)

DEPARTURES
Sheila Scott, British
record-breaking aviator
(1988)

21
OCTOBER

DISH OF THE DAY

Today is International Day of the Nacho, the Mexican dish consisting of layers of melted cheese, tomato salsa, jalapeño peppers, and tortilla chips. Nachos were invented in 1943 by restaurant owner Ignacio "Nacho" Anaya in the city of Piedras Negras. Anaya rustled up the dish to feed some hungry shoppers, named it after himself, and entered into history.

ARRIVALS
Carrie Fisher, American actor who played Princess Leia in *Star Wars* (1956)

DEPARTURES
Horatio Nelson, British naval hero shot on board HMS *Victory* by a French sniper at the Battle of Trafalgar, after refusing to remove his medals that made him an obvious target (1805)

22
OCTOBER

ARRIVALS
Arsène Wenger, French soccer manager (1949)

DEPARTURES
Paul Cézanne, French painter (1906)

Brolly Good Show

In 1797, French balloonist André-Jacques Garnerin makes the first recorded parachute jump, using a giant silk umbrella with a basket below. After being lifted 3,280 feet above Paris by hydrogen balloon, Garnerin severs a tow rope and descends uninjured to the ground. For his next parachute jump, Garnerin is accompanied by a woman, despite police objections that she would faint. She did not.

Light Work

In 1879, American inventor Thomas Edison perfects the first practical electric light bulb, which has a hot, thin filament generating light. Nowadays, such "incandescent" bulbs are being replaced by more eco-friendly LED bulbs. They remain the cartoon symbol for inspiration—a "light bulb moment"—but for how much longer?

23
OCTOBER

ARRIVALS
Michael Crichton, American *Jurassic Park* author (1942)

DEPARTURES
W. G. (William Gilbert) Grace, British cricketing legend (1915)

Pod in Your Pocket

American tech giant Apple launches the iPod in 2001. Previously, people had listened to music on the move using portable cassette tape players (ask a grown-up!). The iPod stores music on a tiny computer hard drive that puts "1,000 songs in your pocket."

Feeling Blue

The Smurfs, small blue-skinned gnome-like creatures, debut in a Belgian children's comic in 1958. The creation of cartoonist Peyo (real name Pierre Culliford), they have since become big movie stars, despite standing just "three apples high."

24
OCTOBER

Referee!

Sheffield FC, the oldest still existing soccer club, is founded in 1857. Back then, the club had its own rules, and games might have as many as 18 players on each side. Players could also catch the ball and push each other, and throw-ins were given to whoever reached the ball first!

Sheep Verse

American children's poet Sarah Josepha Hale is born in 1788. Her most famous poem is "Mary Had a Little Lamb," about a girl followed to school by her pet lamb. The nursery rhyme has inspired many comic versions, including this tongue-twister: "Mary had a little lamb/ It had a sooty foot And everywhere that Mary went/ Its sooty foot it put."

25
OCTOBER

Smart Art

The first artwork produced by artificial intelligence is sold at a New York auction in 2018 for $432,500. Titled *Portrait of Edmond Belamy*, the painting was created by feeding images of 15,000 historic artworks into a computer. Although generated by a computer, the picture is signed—with a complicated mathematical equation.

26
OCTOBER

Airborne

In 1929, Dr Thomas Evans bundles his heavily pregnant wife, Margaret, into a small private airplane and launches into the skies above Miami, Florida, with the sole purpose of having the world's first air-born baby. Twenty minutes later, Margaret gives birth to a little girl whom they later name Airlene.

Not Ok, Really

The Gunfight at the O.K. Corral, the most famous shootout of the American Wild West, takes place in Tombstone, Arizona, in 1881. Four lawmen—including Wyatt Earp and Doc Holliday—battle five outlaws called the Cowboys. The gunfight lasts about 30 seconds and three Cowboys are killed. Despite its name, the fight takes place outside a photographer's studio, not a horse corral (a type of horse enclosure).

27
OCTOBER

Ski-Whizz!
Dolphin Akwa-Skees—the first water skis—are patented in 1925. Though American inventor Fred Waller created water skis—flat, arrow-shaped wooden boards about 8 feet long—he did not invent water skiing. That is credited to American teen Ralph Samuelson, who wore barrel staves on his feet to ski behind a motorboat driven by his brother.

28
OCTOBER

Now You See Me...
This is the day in 1943 on which some UFO researchers say the US Navy made a warship called the USS *Eldridge* disappear before being teleported through time and space and encountering alien life forms. The event is known as the Philadelphia Experiment, after the shipyard where believers say it occurred, but the Navy insists it is a hoax.

Are You a Yahoo?
Famous fantasy novel *Gulliver's Travels* is first published in 1726. Written by Irish author Jonathan Swift, the book describes the adventures of fictional traveler Lemuel Gulliver in many strange lands, including Lilliput, where the 6-inch-tall residents consider him a giant. The book also gives the world the word *yahoo* for a race of rude, brutish humans.

29
OCTOBER

Funnypix
Asterix the Gaul, the feisty warrior with the winged helmet, makes his debut in a French magazine in 1959. Created by writer René Goscinny and cartoonist Albert Uderzo, Asterix and his fellow Gauls have now appeared in almost forty books, the latest in 2019 featuring the modern-sounding characters Selfipix and Binjwatchflix.

Golden Opportunity
In 1904, German-American gymnast George Eyser wins six medals—three gold, two silver, and a bronze—in one day at the Olympic Games in St Louis, Missouri. Eyser's gold medals are for the parallel bars, the long horse vault, and the 25-foot rope climb, and are all the more remarkable because his left leg is wooden.

30
OCTOBER

Meaty Role

The coronation of King Henry VII of England in 1485 marks the start of the Tudor dynasty and the first showing of the Yeoman Warders—nicknamed "Beefeaters," possibly because they receive a large daily ration of beef. Originally royal bodyguards, they still serve the current monarch, and their quaint costumes still bear a Tudor rose.

ARRIVALS
Christopher Wren, British architect of St Paul's Cathedral, London (1632)

DEPARTURES
Henry Dunant, Swiss Red Cross founder (1910)

Don't Panic!

In 1938, American actor and director Orson Welles broadcasts a modern radio version of the sci-fi novel *The War of the Worlds* (by H. G. Wells). The story is delivered in the form of live news broadcasts, and some listeners are fooled into thinking Martian invaders really are attacking Earth; they flee their homes in panic, despite four announcements saying it is just a drama.

31
OCTOBER

Walk, Don't Run

The world's first black-and-white-striped zebra crossing officially goes into use on a road in the English town of Slough in 1951, though earlier trials had used blue and yellow stripes. Many other British road crossings are also named after animals, including the pelican, the puffin, the toucan, and the pegasus (for horse riders).

ARRIVALS
Willow Smith, American singer (2000)

DEPARTURES
Harry Houdini (real name Ehrich Weiss), Hungarian-American magician and world's most famous escape artist (1926)

Stone Face

The carving of Mount Rushmore, featuring the giant heads of four former American presidents, is finally finished in 1941, after 14 years of work. The memorial depicts George Washington, Thomas Jefferson, Theodore Roosevelt, and Abraham Lincoln. There is a secret storeroom hidden behind the head of "Honest Abe."

NUT NIGHT

Tomorrow being All Hallows' Day, this is All Hallows' Eve—better known as Halloween. People tell spooky stories, carve pumpkins, and go trick-or-treating. In Scotland, Halloween is also known as Nut-Crack Night, when young couples place nuts in their shells in hot open fires. If the nuts explode, their relationship is probably doomed.

NOVEMBER

01

NOVEMBER

Looking Up

The amazing painted ceiling of the Sistine Chapel in Vatican City, Rome, is unveiled to the public in 1512. The frescoes took genius artist Michelangelo four years to paint. Contrary to popular belief, Michelangelo painted standing up, not lying on his back.

EAT YOUR GREENS

This is World Vegan Day, an annual celebration of a lifestyle free from animal products. The word *vegan* was invented in the UK in November 1944 by the co-founders of the Vegan Society. *Veg* and *an* are the start and end of the word *vegetarian*, as the society's founders claim that veganism is the logical end result of being vegetarian.

02

NOVEMBER

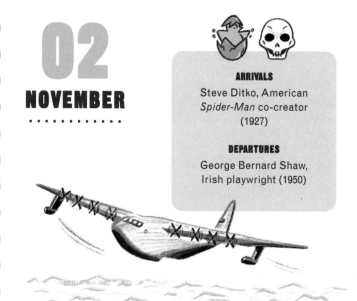

Wood It Fly?

The Hughes H-4 Hercules, the world's largest flying boat, makes its first and only flight in 1947. The giant plane is built largely from wood, and is nicknamed the "Spruce Goose," though in fact it is mostly birch. It takes off and lands on the sea near Los Angeles, its single flight lasting just 26 seconds. Now it just sits in a museum.

Worm Attack!

The internet is hit by its first major computer worm in 1988. American university graduate student Robert Tappan Morris launches a malicious computer program—now known as the Morris worm—which tricks computers into making copies of it. Morris called his program a *worm* after the dragons, or "Great Worms," in the writings of fantasy author J. R. R. Tolkien.

03

NOVEMBER

Dog Star

Sputnik 2, the first spacecraft to carry a mammal into orbit around Earth, is launched by the Soviet Union in 1957. On board is Laika, a husky-like dog found on the streets of Moscow. Laika makes history, but she sadly dies in space, prompting moves to ensure all space animals return to Earth alive in future.

04
NOVEMBER

ARRIVALS
Peter Lord, British *Wallace and Gromit* movies producer (1953)

DEPARTURES
George Klein, Canadian electric wheelchair inventor (1992)

Magic Night

The movie *Harry Potter and the Philosopher's Stone*, based on J. K. Rowling's bestseller, has its world premiere in London in 2001. Amazingly, none of the eight *Harry Potter* movies has won a coveted Academy Award in any category, despite being the third most successful movie franchise, after the Marvel Cinematic Universe and *Star Wars*.

Cashing In

American bar owner James Ritty is granted a patent for his new invention, the cash register, in 1879. He created the device in an attempt to stop employees pocketing his profits by forcing them to register cash sales—hence the name—with a bell ringing each time they did. He called it "Ritty's Incorruptible Cashier."

05
NOVEMBER

ARRIVALS
John Alcock, British pilot who was the first to fly non-stop across the Atlantic Ocean (1892)

DEPARTURES
James Clerk Maxwell, Scottish scientist who came up with the theory of electromagnetism (1879)

FALL GUY

In the UK, this is Bonfire Night, celebrating the foiling of the Gunpowder Plot back in 1605. The attempt to blow up King James I and London's House of Lords ended when conspirator Guy Fawkes was discovered in a cellar with 36 barrels of gunpowder and a lighted lantern. Effigies of Fawkes have been burned on bonfires ever since, and fireworks fill the skies on this night.

06
NOVEMBER

Out for the Count

According to 1897 horror novel *Dracula* by Irish author Bram Stoker, this is the day when the blood-sucking count dies after a battle in his creepy castle in Transylvania. Count Dracula is turned to dust not with a wooden stake through his heart—as in the many movie versions of the story—but with a bowie knife. Oh, and his head gets chopped off too.

ARRIVALS
Adolphe Sax, Belgian saxophone inventor (1814)

DEPARTURES
Kate Greenaway, British children's book illustrator (1901)

123

07

NOVEMBER

ARRIVALS

Marie Curie, Polish-French Nobel Prize-winning scientist (1867)

DEPARTURES

Cornelis Drebbel, Dutch submarine inventor (1633)

Big Hit with the Locals

With a small boy the only witness, a meteorite falls from the skies to strike a wheat field in Ensisheim, France, in 1492—making it the oldest meteorite with a known date of impact. Weighing 280 pounds, the big green stone makes a crater over 3 feet deep. So many people—including the King of Austria—want a piece of it, that less than half remains today.

Swing Bridge

In 1940, heavy gusting winds set a suspension bridge swinging across the Tacoma Narrows strait in the state of Washington, USA. The wobbly bridge, nicknamed "Galloping Gertie," is only four months old, and at 11 a.m., it sways so violently that it collapses into the water below. Luckily, no one is hurt. You can find film of the disaster on the internet.

08

NOVEMBER

ARRIVALS

Gordon Ramsay, British celebrity chef (1966)

DEPARTURES

Chad Varah, British Samaritans charity founder (2007)

Yeti or Not?

In 1951, three mountaineers on the lower slopes of Mount Everest in Nepal find a line of strange footprints in the snow. The native Nepalese climber in the group immediately identifies them as belonging to a "yeti" or "abominable snowman." Photographs show that the 12-inch-long tracks have one giant toe and three small toes, and are unlike any known wildlife.

The Frogs of War

One of the world's strangest wars occurs in Malaysia in 1970 between two massive armies of frogs—one comprising green frogs, and the other brown, gray, and yellow frogs. The two armies fight in their thousands over a 16-foot-wide puddle in what is later thought to be a breeding frenzy. Sadly, some frogs, er, croaked.

09

NOVEMBER

HAPPY UNBIRTHDAY

Today is Cambodia's national day. The South-East Asian nation is home to the temple of Angkor Wat, the world's largest religious monument, which also features on its flag. Unusually, Cambodians do not celebrate their birthdays, but if a gift is given it should not be wrapped in white paper, as white is associated with funerals.

ARRIVALS

Carl Sagan, American astronomer (1934)

DEPARTURES

Dylan Thomas, Welsh poet (1953)

10 NOVEMBER

Diamond Geezer

In 1958, New York jeweler Harry Winston donates a large blue diamond to the Smithsonian Institution in Washington DC, USA, by popping it into the post. The Hope Diamond, as it is known, is now valued at over $200 million. The diamond had many previous owners, despite claims of a deadly curse. Luckily, Harry lives another 20 years.

ARRIVALS
Neil Gaiman, British
Coraline author (1960)

DEPARTURES
Gideon Mantell, British
fossil hunter who named
Iguanodon (1852)

11 NOVEMBER

PEACE AT LAST

Many countries celebrate Armistice Day, this being the day on which the First World War formally ended in 1918. The treaty between the Allied and German armies was signed at 5:45 a.m. but didn't come into force until 11 a.m.: the eleventh hour of the eleventh day of the eleventh month. The red poppy as a symbol of remembrance—the idea of American professor Moina Michael—was adopted internationally in 1921.

ARRIVALS
Leonardo DiCaprio,
American actor (1974)

DEPARTURES
Lili'uokalani, last queen
of the Hawaiian Kingdom
(1917)

12 NOVEMBER

Whale Fail

On a beach in Oregon, USA, in 1970, a rotting dead sperm whale is dynamited in an effort to destroy it. Far too much explosive is used, rocketing lumps of stinky blubber over spectators. When the blast clears, most of the whale remains and has to be buried. Decades later, the epic fail becomes an Internet video watched by millions.

ARRIVALS
Auguste Rodin, French
sculptor (1840)

DEPARTURES
Stan Lee, American
superhero comics
creator (2018)

Tight Fit

French acrobat Jules Léotard performs the first flying trapeze act at a circus in Paris in 1859. His death-defying aerial routine makes him famous, as does his tight one-piece costume. Known now as a leotard, the garment proves popular, along with leg warmers, during the dance fitness craze of the 1980s.

13
NOVEMBER

KIND OF NICE

This is World Kindness Day, an international celebration of niceness started in 1998. Countries across the world take part, with past kindness events including handing out thousands of chocolate bars and flowers, a kindness flash mob, and a mass Kindness Hug on Bondi Beach in Sydney, Australia. Who will you be nice to?

ARRIVALS
Robert Louis Stevenson, Scottish *Treasure Island* author (1850)

DEPARTURES
Elsa Schiaparelli, Italian fashion designer (1973)

14
NOVEMBER

Whale of a Tale

Classic novel *Moby-Dick* by American author Herman Melville is first published in 1851. It recounts the hunt by crazed whaling-ship boss Captain Ahab for a giant white whale that once bit off his leg. It ends badly for Ahab and most of his crew, though one character—chief mate Starbuck—goes on to lend his name to a chain of coffee shops.

ARRIVALS
Andy Stanton, British *Mr Gum* series children's author (1973)

DEPARTURES
Georg Wilhelm Steller, German naturalist with a sea lion and a sea cow named after him (1746)

Flight Deck

In 1910, American flying pioneer Eugene Ely becomes the first person to successfully launch an airplane from a ship. Ely pilots his primitive plane down a long ramp on the deck of the warship USS *Birmingham*, before plunging many feet down to the sea, skimming its surface and landing on a nearby beach, his goggles drenched with spray.

15
NOVEMBER

ARRIVALS
Georgia O'Keeffe, American artist (1887)

DEPARTURES
Johannes Kepler, German astronomer (1630)

X Marks the Box

Tech company Microsoft launches its Xbox video game console in 2001. It proves hugely popular and sells over 24 million units before being retired in 2009.

16
NOVEMBER

Get the Message

In 1974, the Arecibo radio telescope in Puerto Rico transmits a radio message into space that carries information about humans and our home planet, Earth. The message—including a simple illustration of a person—is aimed at a distant cluster of stars known as M13 and will reach it in roughly 25,000 years' time. Don't wait up for a reply. Sadly, a few of its structures started falling off in 2020, and in November of that year the entire telescope collapsed.

17
NOVEMBER

ARRIVALS
Terry, Cairn Terrier who played Toto in the movie *The Wizard of Oz* (1933)

DEPARTURES
Catherine the Great, Russian empress (1796)

Mouse in the House

In 1970, American inventor Douglas Engelbart is granted a patent for the device we call a computer mouse. Engelbart had been working on the idea for several years and originally called his wheeled screen-pointer a "bug." The name *mouse* arose because the cord at its rear made it look like a long-tailed rodent.

First Van on the Moon

Lunokhod 1, the first wheeled vehicle to move on a surface outside Earth, lands on the moon in 1970. Looking like a large tin bath on wheels, it is controlled remotely by the Soviet Union, with solar panels powering its movements. Its name means "moonwalker" in Russian, and it is, of course, still up there, going nowhere.

18
NOVEMBER

ARRIVALS
Wolfgang Joop, German JOOP! fashion company founder (1944)

DEPARTURES
Jacques Anquetil, French cyclist nicknamed "Monsieur Chrono" (1987)

Crafty

Popular computer game *Minecraft* is officially released in 2011, having been in development by its Swedish creator Markus "Notch" Persson for over two years. Persson originally called it "Cave Game" before settling on the title *Minecraft*.

127

19
NOVEMBER

FEELING FLUSH?

This is World Toilet Day. While the idea
sounds funny, the day was designated by the
United Nations to highlight the more than
four billion people in the world who don't
have access to safe, clean ways of dealing
with their wastes. Think of them next time
you go. And remember to wash your hands.

Need a Wii?

Japanese technology giant Nintendo launches
its Wii games console in the USA in 2006, before
rolling it out worldwide. Originally codenamed
"Revolution," the name Wii was finally chosen
because the two lower-case *i*'s are meant to
represent two players side by side, while *Wii* as
a word is easy to remember in any language.

20
NOVEMBER

On Your Bike

In 1866, Pierre Lallement, a French mechanic in
the USA, is granted a patent for a pedal-driven
vehicle with two large wooden wheels and a seat
supported on a springy strip of metal. Lallement's
invention—an early forerunner of the modern
bicycle—is nicknamed the "boneshaker" because
it is so uncomfortable to ride.

On Your Saucer

In 1952, Polish-American UFO fan George
Adamski claims to have made direct contact
with a Venusian UFO pilot called Orthon in
the Colorado Desert, California. Sadly, Orthon
refuses to be photographed, but Adamski later
says he was humanoid with long blond hair
and reddish shoes, though "his trousers were
not like mine."

21
NOVEMBER

No Link

In 1953, a group of English
scientists reveal that the so-called
Piltdown Man fossils—supposedly
those of a "missing link" between
apes and humans—are in fact
a hoax constructed 40 years earlier
using an orangutan jawbone and
a bit of stained human skull.
To this day, no one is sure
who faked the fossils.

22
NOVEMBER

ARRIVALS
Billie Jean King,
American tennis player
(1943)

DEPARTURES
C. S. (Clive Staples)
Lewis, British *The
Chronicles of Narnia*
series author (1963)

Not So Jolly Roger

English pirate Edward Teach—better known as Blackbeard—meets his end in 1718 in a battle with British Royal Navy forces just off the coast of North Carolina, USA. Blackbeard did indeed have a long black beard, which he braided into pigtails and tied with ribbons. He also tucked fiery fuses under his hat to scare his enemies.

Story Time

The world's first entirely computer-animated movie, *Toy Story*, is released in the USA in 1995. It famously tells the tale of a group of toys trying to rescue missing space ranger Buzz Lightyear, but in early versions of the script Buzz was called Lunar Larry and Sheriff Woody Pride was a villainous ventriloquist's dummy.

23
NOVEMBER

ARRIVALS
William Bonney,
American Wild West
outlaw known as "Billy
the Kid" (1859)

DEPARTURES
Roald Dahl, British
children's author
(1990)

World Record

The first jukebox is installed in the Palais Royale Saloon in San Francisco, USA, in 1889. Customers insert a nickel into the coin-in-the-slot machine to listen to music played from a revolving cylinder through one of four stethoscope-like tubes. The price gave rise to the nickname "nickelodeon," though the bar closed within a year.

Doctor New

Long-running sci-fi show *Doctor Who* debuts on British TV screens in 1963. The first Doctor is played by William Hartnell as a grumpy old man, with his granddaughter Susan as his time-traveling companion. Viewers had to wait until series two for the arrival of evil pepperpot-shaped villains the Daleks.

24
NOVEMBER

Galloping Success

Black Beauty, one of the world's bestselling and best-loved novels, is published in the UK in 1877. It is unusual in being narrated by a horse, and its full title is *Black Beauty: His Grooms and Companions; The Autobiography of a Horse, "Translated from the Original Equine by Anna Sewell"*—which is almost a novel in itself.

ARRIVALS
Frances Hodgson
Burnett, British-
American *The Secret
Garden* author
(1849)

DEPARTURES
Dodie Smith, British
*The Hundred and One
Dalmatians* author
(1990)

NOVEMBER

25
NOVEMBER

ARRIVALS
Joe DiMaggio, American baseball player (1914)

DEPARTURES
Al Plastino, American co-creator of Supergirl comic character (2013)

Monkey Business

According to classic 1968 sci-fi movie *Planet of the Apes*, this is the day in the year 3978 when human astronauts crash-land on a strange planet only to find that it is run by gorillas, orangutans, and chimps with the power of speech.

Good Boy

The Alexandria "Blue Boy" Postmaster's Provisional—one of the world's rarest postage stamps—is mailed in 1847. Issued in Virginia, USA, the circular blue stamp is attached to an envelope containing a love letter that ends with the instruction "Burn as usual." Luckily it survived, and it sold in 2019 for $1.18 million.

26
NOVEMBER

ARRIVALS
Charles M. Schulz, American *Peanuts* comic strip creator (1922)

DEPARTURES
Stephen Hillenburg, American *SpongeBob SquarePants* creator (2018)

Tomb Raider

In 1922, British archeologist Howard Carter, accompanied by aristocrat Lord Carnarvon, makes a small hole in the wall of an ancient tomb in Egypt's Valley of the Kings and peers through by candlelight. Carnarvon asks, "Can you see anything?" "Yes, wonderful things!" Carter replies, having found the tomb of the pharaoh Tutankhamun (opened on February 16th, 1923).

Peace Time

At 5:10 p.m. in 1977, TV viewers in southern England have their local news taken over by a six-minute message from "Vrillon," who claims to represent the Ashtar Galactic Command and suggests that humans should embrace peace. To this day, no one has admitted to the prank. Maybe it was real.

27
NOVEMBER

Knock Knock

In 1809, a deluge of callers turns up at 54 Berners Street, London, to the surprise of the occupants. The crowd includes chimney sweeps, coalmen, bakers, doctors, lawyers, vicars, and even the Lord Mayor of London. All had been sent letters asking them to attend by hoaxer Theodore Hook, who had bet a friend that he could make any address famous. It worked!

ARRIVALS
Bruce Lee, American-Hongkonger martial arts movie star (1940)

DEPARTURES
Ada Lovelace, British computing pioneer (1852)

28 NOVEMBER

RED LETTER DAY

If there is life on Mars, today it should party. Here on Earth, this is Red Planet Day, in honor of our little rocky, rusty neighbor. Both planets have days of similar length, with a Mars day just 39 minutes longer. However, a Mars year has 687 days compared to Earth's 365, meaning that for Mars, this book would be a whole lot longer!

ARRIVALS
Luke Howard, British inventor of cloud names (1772)

DEPARTURES
Matsuo Basho, Japanese haiku poet (1694)

29 NOVEMBER

ARRIVALS
Lauren Child, British *Charlie and Lola* series author and illustrator (1965)

DEPARTURES
Giacomo Puccini, Italian opera composer (1924)

SPOT ON

This is International Jaguar Day, highlighting the many threats to the survival of these beautiful spotty big cats. Jaguars are found only in the Americas, from Mexico to Argentina. The national rugby team of Argentina has a jaguar as its emblem. However, the team are mistakenly nicknamed "Los Pumas" (the pumas).

What a Pong

American company Atari announces its first arcade video game, *Pong*, in 1972. *Pong* is a simple two-dimensional video version of table tennis, where players bat an electronic puck back and forth with paddles. Despite being such a simple game, the original arcade machines are now considered collector's items.

30 NOVEMBER

ARRIVALS
Winston Churchill, British Second World War prime minister (1874)

DEPARTURES
Oscar Wilde, Irish playwright (1900)

Big Draw

The world's first international soccer match takes place at a cricket ground in Glasgow, Scotland, in 1872, attracting a crowd of four thousand people. The game is between the national teams of England and Scotland and finishes as a 0–0 draw, despite November 30th also being the feast day of Scotland's patron saint, Andrew.

DECEMBER

01
DECEMBER

XMAS COUNTDOWN

Today many people around the world will be opening the first window on their Advent calendar, the start of a 24-day countdown to Christmas. The modern printed Advent calendar was invented by German Gerhard Lang, and first sold in 1908. Lang went on to make many different versions, including the first with chocolate treats in 1926.

ARRIVALS
Madame Tussaud, French artist famous for waxworks (1761)

DEPARTURES
- Stéphane Grappelli, French jazz violinist (1997)

Hungry Henry

In 1135, King Henry I of England suffers one of the most unusual ends of any monarch—not in battle or by being beheaded, but through overeating a big dish of primitive eel-like fish known as lampreys. His doctor has advised him against it, but Henry scoffs the lot and dies as a result.

Pep Talk

American soft drink Dr Pepper is patented in 1885. It is the creation of pharmacist Charles Alderton and is first served at a drugstore in Waco, Texas. Dr Pepper's unique flavor stems from a secret recipe, while a similar mystery surrounds its name. Many theories exist, but it may simply be that the drink "peps" you up.

02
DECEMBER

Coo!

In 1943, three British homing pigeons—White Vision, Winkie, and Tyke—become the first recipients of the Dickin Medal, the animal equivalent of the Victoria Cross medal for bravery. All three birds flew huge distances to alert rescuers to the positions of aircraft that had crashed into the sea, enabling their crews to be recovered safely.

ARRIVALS
Britney Spears, American pop singer (1981)

DEPARTURES
Dame Alicia Markova, British ballerina (2004)

Chinese Takeaway

Puyi, a two-year-old boy, becomes China's last emperor in 1908. He is taken screaming from his parents and placed on the Dragon Throne in the Forbidden City, Beijing, against his will. The infant emperor is considered divine, and no one can control him, so he quickly becomes incredibly spoiled. His reign ends in 1912.

03
DECEMBER

Snow Joke
In 2018, Dane Best, a nine-year-old resident of Severance, Colorado, USA, asks local officials to overturn a hundred-year-old ban on snowballing, arguing that the town's children "want the opportunity to have a snowball fight like the rest of the world." The officials agree, and the mayor goes outside and makes him a snowball.

ARRIVALS
John Wallis, British mathematician who invented the infinity symbol: ∞ (1616)

DEPARTURES
Auguste Renoir, French painter (1919)

Play Time
The first Sony PlayStation video game console goes on sale in Japan in 1994. It was developed by electronics engineer Ken Kutaragi, and is the first console to sell over 100 million units. One of the most popular early games for the system is *Crash Bandicoot*, though the title character was originally going to be a wombat called Willy.

04
DECEMBER

ARRIVALS
Jay-Z (real name Shawn Carter), American hip-hop rapper (1969)

DEPARTURES
Arnold Lobel, American *Frog and Toad* series author (1987)

Ghost Ship
In 1872, American merchant ship *Mary Celeste* is found drifting in the Atlantic Ocean, close to the Azores, by a passing Canadian vessel. The entire crew are missing, but what happened to them remains a mystery. Theories include a tornado, an attack by a giant squid, or a hasty abandoning of the ship to avoid an explosion.

05
DECEMBER

ARRIVALS
Walt Disney, American *Mickey Mouse* creator and cartoon company boss (1901)

DEPARTURES
Wolfgang Amadeus Mozart, Austrian composer (1791)

Dab Hand
In 1996, Maciej Henneberg, a Polish-Australian forensic scientist at the University of Adelaide, Australia, reveals his discovery that humans and koalas have almost identical fingerprints. As a result, he warns: "Although it is extremely unlikely that koala prints would be found at the scene of a crime, police should at least be aware of the possibility."

06
DECEMBER

ARRIVALS
Nick Park, British *Wallace and Gromit* creator (1958)

DEPARTURES
Johnny Hallyday (real name Jean-Philippe Léo Smet), French singer who brought rock 'n' roll to France (2017)

Record Recording

In 1877, American inventor Thomas Edison makes the first ever sound recording using his latest invention, the phonograph. Vibrations made by his voice cut grooves in a rotating cylinder of metal foil, which he plays back to hear himself reciting "Mary Had a Little Lamb." As he later recalled, "I was never so taken aback in my life."

FINN FUN

The people of Finland celebrate their independence today by flying their blue and white flag and baking cakes with patriotic icing. Families also eagerly watch the country's most popular TV show—live coverage of a glittering reception held at the Presidential Palace in Helsinki, with celebrity guests drinking punch made to a secret recipe.

07
DECEMBER

ARRIVALS
Anne Fine, British *Madame Doubtfire* children's author (1947)

DEPARTURES
Thomas Nast, American cartoonist famous for his drawings of Santa Claus (1902)

What a 'Nana

At about 1:45 p.m. today in 2019, Georgian-American artist David Datuna removes a banana duct-taped to an art gallery wall in Miami, Florida, and eats it. The banana is actually part of a work titled *Comedian* by another artist, Maurizio Cattelan, and valued at $120,000. Datuna claims his action is an art performance called *Hungry Artist*.

Speedy Work

In 1667, Danish astronomer Ole Rømer becomes the first person to calculate the speed of light. He figures it out after observing changes in how long it took light to reach Earth from one of Jupiter's moons. Light travels at about 186,000 miles per second, and takes 8 minutes, 20 seconds to get here from the sun.

08
DECEMBER

ARRIVALS
Diego Rivera, Mexican mural artist (1886)

DEPARTURES
Antônio Carlos Jobim, Brazilian bossa nova musician (1994)

First Contact

In 1733, a Mr James Cracker of the village of Fleet in Dorset, England, looks up to see a silvery disk flying above him in the sky in broad daylight. According to his eyewitness account, it darted about, and "shot with speed like a star falling in the night." His is the first recorded sighting of what we now call a UFO.

DECEMBER

09
DECEMBER

ARRIVALS
Jean de Brunhoff, French
Babar the Elephant creator
(1899)

DEPARTURES
Norman Joseph Woodland,
American co-inventor
of the barcode
(2012)

Green for Go

The first traffic light is installed outside the British Houses of Parliament in London in 1868. The gas-lit light has red and green lamps for night use as well as protruding semaphore arms, which are operated by a policeman who turns them to face the horse-drawn traffic. Sadly, the light explodes in January due to a gas leak.

Fake Fir

A Charlie Brown Christmas, the first TV cartoon special featuring the *Peanuts* characters of Charles M. Schulz (see October 2nd), airs on American TV in 1965. In the story, Charlie Brown takes pity on a real but scraggy fir tree, preferring it to a fake tree made of aluminum. Within a few years, sales of aluminum trees in America almost vanished.

10
DECEMBER

ARRIVALS
Ada Lovelace, British
computing pioneer (1815)

DEPARTURES
Alfred Nobel, Swedish
dynamite inventor and
Nobel Prize founder (1896)

It's a Fact

The first volume of the now world-famous reference book *Encyclopaedia Britannica* goes on sale in 1768. The fact-packed book is published in three volumes by a company based in Edinburgh, which is why the work has a thistle—Scotland's national flower—as its logo.

Meet the Metre

In 1799, France becomes the world's first country to adopt the metric system of weights and measures, including the meter—originally defined as one ten-millionth of the distance over the Earth's surface from the equator to the North Pole. Today only three nations don't use the metric system—Liberia, Myanmar, and the USA.

11
DECEMBER

ARRIVALS
Marco Pierre White,
British celebrity chef
(1961)

DEPARTURES
Ravi Shankar, Indian sitar
musician (2012)

Bird Brains

The video game *Angry Birds* is released in America in 2009 by Finnish company Rovio. Players catapult multicolored wingless birds at hungry green pigs, which are hiding after stealing the birds' eggs. Pigs were chosen as the birds' enemies because swine flu was in the news at the time.

12
DECEMBER

Hover Bother

British inventor Christopher Cockerell patents his design for a hovercraft in 1955. He builds working models from cans and hair dryers and tries to get funding from the military. However, the Navy says the hovercraft is a plane, the Air Force says it is a boat, and the Army just isn't interested. Luckily, he gets help elsewhere.

Dozens of People

In 2012, people around the world celebrate this date as being the last in the twentieth century with the same number for the day, month, and year: 12-12-12. Many couples choose it as a memorable day to get married, while others think the world has been predicted to end on this day. Breaking news: it didn't.

13
DECEMBER

ON THE FIDDLE

This is World Violin Day, a global celebration of the four-stringed fiddle. The most famous maker is Italian craftsman Antonio Stradivari, whose 300-year-old instruments are today worth huge sums. The so-called Messiah Stradivarius—one of about five hundred "Strads" still surviving—is worth about $20 million and lives in a British museum, though some say it is a fake.

STAR ATTRACTION

Today is St Lucia's Day, celebrated in Sweden by girls wearing long white dresses with trailing red belts, sticking wreaths of lighted candles on their heads, and serenading people with Christmas songs. Other children dress as gnomes, giant gingerbread men, and "star boys"—with even some dogs donning fancy dress too!

14
DECEMBER

Last Men on the Moon

In 1972, American *Apollo 17* astronauts Eugene Cernan and Harrison Schmitt become the last humans to walk on the moon, so far. The pair spend three days carrying out experiments and driving around in a moon buggy. Cernan is last off the lunar surface, leaving behind his daughter Tracy's initials, written in moondust.

15
DECEMBER

Quiz Time

Brain-busting board game *Trivial Pursuit* is invented in 1979 by Canadians Chris Haney and Scott Abbott. *Trivial Pursuit* is now a worldwide bestseller, despite endless arguments over whether the playing pieces are called "wedges" or "cheeses."

ARRIVALS
Gustav Eiffel, French Eiffel Tower engineer (1832)

DEPARTURES
Walt Disney, American *Mickey Mouse* creator and cartoon company boss (1966) (see May 15th)

16
DECEMBER

ARRIVALS
Quentin Blake, British children's book illustrator and author (1932)

DEPARTURES
Colonel Harland Sanders, American Kentucky Fried Chicken founder (1980)

Blow Your Top

In 1707, Japan's Mount Fuji—actually two active volcanoes—erupts for the last recorded time. The two-week-long eruption throws ash, rock, and cinders into the air, making the sky so dark that the citizens of Edo (now Tokyo), 60 miles away, have to use candles during the day. No one knows when it might erupt again.

LET ME IN

In Mexico, this is the first day of Las Posadas, a traditional Christmas festival. *Posadas* is Spanish for "lodgings." For the next nine days, a gathering of children dressed as Mary, Joseph, shepherds, and angels asks for entry at a different household for the night. When they are finally let in, they share festive foods and smash a star-shaped piñata.

17
DECEMBER

ARRIVALS
Jacqueline Wilson, British *Tracy Beaker* series children's author (1945)

DEPARTURES
Francis Beaufort, Irish creator of the Beaufort wind scale (1857)

The Wright Stuff

History is made in the Kill Devil Hills of North Carolina, USA, in 1903 when former bicycle-maker Orville Wright pilots the *Wright Flyer I*, an aircraft built with his brother Wilbur, for a distance of about 120 feet. The flight lasts just 12 seconds but is the first by a human in a steerable, powered, heavier-than-air plane.

Massive Mystery

In 1790, a giant stone sculpture nearly 12 feet wide and almost 40 inches thick is found buried in a square in Mexico City. Known today as the Aztec Sun Stone, it is the most famous remaining artwork of the lost Aztec Empire of centuries earlier. It is elaborately decorated, but no one is sure what the symbols actually mean.

18
DECEMBER

ARRIVALS
Steven Spielberg, American film director (1946)

DEPARTURES
Richard Owen, British scientist who coined the word *dinosaur* (1892)

Nuts

Festive ballet *The Nutcracker*, with music by Russian composer Tchaikovsky, premieres in St Petersburg in 1892. Some critics are not impressed with the story of toys that come alive on Christmas Eve, one complaining that "the entire stage is filled with children," and adding, "In large amounts this is unbearable."

Green Meanie

Classic cartoon *How the Grinch Stole Christmas!* airs on American TV for the first time in 1966. It tells how meanie Mr Grinch tries to steal Christmas from the residents of Whoville, but fails because of their festive spirit. However, in the original book by Dr Seuss there is one big difference—the Grinch isn't green, he's black and white with pink eyes.

19
DECEMBER

ARRIVALS
Robert B. Sherman, American *Mary Poppins* film songwriter (1925)

DEPARTURES
J. M. W. (Joseph Mallord William) Turner, British landscape painter (1851)

Radio Star

The first ever radio broadcast from space is sent from an orbiting American satellite in 1958. An on-board tape recorder carries a message from American president Dwight Eisenhower: "Through this unique means I convey to you and all mankind America's wish for peace on Earth and goodwill toward men everywhere."

Grave Mistake

The novel *A Christmas Carol* by British author Charles Dickens is first published in 1843, telling how miserly Ebenezer Scrooge is visited by ghosts on Christmas Eve. The character was inspired by a real person whose name Dickens saw on a gravestone: Ebenezer Lennox Scroggie. Scroggie was described as a "meal man"—a corn merchant—which Dickens misread as "mean man."

20
DECEMBER

NIGHT LIGHT

In Iran and other former Persian countries, tonight is Yalda Night, a celebration of the longest and darkest night of the year—the winter solstice in the northern hemisphere. Friends and family gather to read poetry and share watermelons and pomegranates, whose red flesh symbolizes the coming light of dawn.

ARRIVALS
Bob de Moor (real name Robert Frans Marie De Moor), Belgian comics artist (1925)

DEPARTURES
Carl Sagan, American astronomer (1996)

DECEMBER

21
DECEMBER

ARRIVALS
Jack Russell, British priest and dog breeder who developed the Jack Russell terrier (1795)

DEPARTURES
F. (Francis) Scott Fitzgerald, American Jazz Age author (1940)

One Across

The first newspaper crossword puzzle appears in the *New York World* in 1913. Invented by British-American journalist Arthur Wynne, it is originally called a "word-cross" and has no black squares. Today, crosswords are compiled in many languages, with Italian apparently the hardest to set clues in, because so many words end in a vowel.

DAY OF THE DALEKS

"EXTERMINATE!" Or should that be "CELEBRATE!"? Today is International Dalek Remembrance Day, celebrating the scary robot mutant monsters from the British sci-fi TV series *Doctor Who*. The Daleks debuted in 1963, and were invented by writer Terry Nation, who said the name just "rolled off the typewriter."

22
DECEMBER

ARRIVALS
Ralph Fiennes, British actor who played Lord Voldemort in the *Harry Potter* movies (1962)

DEPARTURES
Beatrix Potter, British children's author (1943)

Light Bulb Moment

In 1882, American inventor Edward H. Johnson creates the first electric Christmas tree lights at his home in New York City. He has 80 walnut-sized bulbs specially made for him in red, white, and blue—the colors of the American flag—and is known today as the "Father of Electric Christmas Tree Lights."

23
DECEMBER

ARRIVALS
Akihito, 125th Japanese emperor (1933)

DEPARTURES
Pierre Jules Janssen, French astronomer who discovered helium (1907)

Highly Fishy

In 1938, a strange fish, thought to have been extinct since the time of the dinosaurs 66 million years ago, is caught off the coast of South Africa. Known from fossils, the fish is a coelacanth, a slow-moving creature that lives deep in the ocean and has since been filmed happily swimming upside down and backward.

24 DECEMBER

First Night

Christmas carol "Silent Night" is premiered in St Nicholas Church, Oberndorf, Austria, in 1818. The lyrics by Joseph Mohr, a young priest, are set to a guitar accompaniment by organist Franz Xaver Gruber, as the church's organ has been damaged by floods. Bing Crosby's 1935 version is the fourth-bestselling single of all time.

Christmas Angel

The *Angel of the North*, a 65-foot-tall steel sculpture near Gateshead, UK, is the victim of a fun stunt in 2018. Overnight, a giant Santa hat is placed on the head of the winged figure by a gang of pranksters. It stays there for five days, until they return to remove it, with one of the gang disguised as the Grinch.

ARRIVALS
John, still unpopular King of England (1166) (see June 15th)

DEPARTURES
Elisabeth Beresford, British *The Wombles* author (2010)

25 DECEMBER

Peace Time

On Christmas Day, 1914, early on in the First World War, many British and German troops along the Western Front in France hold an unofficial ceasefire and venture into "no man's land" between their opposing trenches to swap Christmas greetings and small gifts. Some also say a soccer match was played, which the Germans won 3–2.

ARRIVALS
Muhammad Ali Jinnah, founder of Pakistan (1876)

DEPARTURES
Charlie Chaplin, British silent-film star (1977)

Watch Out

Though an electronic watch is a common Christmas gift nowadays, 50 years ago it was an amazing technological breakthrough. In 1969 Japanese company Seiko unveils its Astron wristwatch, the world's first "quartz clock" watch. However, it isn't cheap, costing the equivalent of about $10,000 in today's money.

Beat That

In 1956, Ritchie Starkey, a teenage boy living in Liverpool, UK, gets a second-hand drum kit as a present from his stepdad, Harry. The noise of Ritchie practicing soon annoys the neighbors, who don't know that he will change his name to Ringo Starr, join pop group the Beatles, and become the world's most famous drummer.

141

26
DECEMBER

BOX CLEVER

This is Boxing Day in Britain—traditionally a day in which servants and tradespeople were given a box containing money or gifts as a "thank you" for their service. Many former parts of the British Empire also celebrate, including Bermuda, where Gombey dancers in colorful costumes and painted masks dance through the streets.

ARRIVALS
Charles Babbage, British computer pioneer (1791)

DEPARTURES
Gerry Anderson, British *Thunderbirds* TV show creator (2012)

27
DECEMBER

ARRIVALS
Louis Pasteur, French microbiologist who invented pasteurization (1822)

DEPARTURES
Carrie Fisher, American actor who played Princess Leia in *Star Wars* (2016)

Fairy Tale Beginning

The play *Peter Pan; or, the Boy Who Wouldn't Grow Up* debuts in London in 1904. It was written by Scottish author J. M. Barrie who, 25 years later, generously gives his copyright in *Peter Pan* to the Great Ormond Street Hospital for Sick Children in London, to help raise money for their work.

Thumbs Up

Once the world's largest building, the Hagia Sophia cathedral in Istanbul, Turkey, opens in 537 CE. Its name means "holy wisdom" in Latin, and it is now a much-visited mosque. Inside is a pillar with a hole where visitors insert their thumb, make a wish, and spin in a circle in the hope their wish comes true.

28
DECEMBER

ARRIVALS
Stan Lee, American superhero comics creator (1922)

DEPARTURES
Maurice Ravel, French composer (1937)

Dish of the Day

In 1886, Josephine Cochran, a wealthy woman from Shelbyville, Illinois, USA, is granted a patent for the first automatic dish-washing machine. Cochran was tired of servants breaking her best china, so she built a device that squirted dirty dishes with hot soapy water while they sat safely in wire compartments.

Hit for Six

The highest ever score in a first-class cricket game is recorded in 1926. Victoria plays New South Wales at the Melbourne Cricket Ground, Australia, and scores 1,017, to win by an innings and 656 runs. However, in the return match against New South Wales, Victoria are all out for just 35 runs in their first innings.

29
DECEMBER

COLD SPOT

Today Mongolia celebrates its independence. Mongolia is a large landlocked country in eastern Asia and has the world's coldest capital city—Ulaanbaatar—with an average annual temperature of just below freezing. Many citizens live in tents called *gers*, and right now it could be as cold as −13 degrees Fahrenheit outside.

ARRIVALS
Charles Macintosh, Scottish raincoat inventor (1766)

DEPARTURES
Christina Rossetti, British "In the Bleak Midwinter" poet (1894)

30
DECEMBER

ARRIVALS
Asa Griggs Candler, American developer of Coca-Cola (1851)

DEPARTURES
Amelia Jenks Bloomer, American women's rights activist, after whom "bloomers" (trousers) are named (1894)

Where Did the Day Go?

In 2011, in the South Pacific island state of Samoa, December 30th simply disappears. At the end of December 29th, Samoa skips straight to December 31st, moving the imaginary line where days are said to start and end on Earth so that Samoa is on the other side of it. As a result, Samoa is now one of the first places to see in the coming New Year.

Bending the Truth

In 1930, American Army Air Corps officer Albert William Stevens takes a photograph while 72,395 feet above South Dakota, which shows the curvature of the Earth's horizon for the first time. Despite this, and the fact that Earth's shadow on the moon is circular during a lunar eclipse, some people still flatly insist the Earth is, er, flat.

31
DECEMBER

ARRIVALS
Henri Matisse, French artist (1869)

DEPARTURES
Old Father Time, passing away at the stroke of midnight...

GOOD LUCK!

In the calendar used across most of the world, this is New Year's Eve, the turn of the year being marked with parties and midnight fireworks. However, some countries also celebrate this as St Sylvester's Day, and in Austria—where pigs are considered lucky—people give each other marzipan pigs, as well as toadstools, horseshoes, and four-leaf clovers.

143

TRADE MARK CREDITS